BLOOM
WHEREVER GOD PLANTS YOU

Following Jesus from a small
Caribbean Parish to the
BIG APPLE

J. MASTINE NISBETT

Foreword by: The Rt. Reverend Theodore A. Daniels D.D.

authorHOUSE®

AuthorHouse™
1663 Liberty Drive
Bloomington, IN 47403
www.authorhouse.com
Phone: 1 (800) 839-8640

© 2019 J. MASTINE NISBETT. All rights reserved.

No part of this book may be reproduced, stored in a retrieval system, or transmitted by any means without the written permission of the author.

Published by AuthorHouse 10/30/2019

ISBN: 978-1-7283-3338-0 (sc)
ISBN: 978-1-7283-3336-6 (hc)
ISBN: 978-1-7283-3337-3 (e)

Library of Congress Control Number: 2019917280

Print information available on the last page.

Any people depicted in stock imagery provided by Getty Images are models, and such images are being used for illustrative purposes only. Certain stock imagery © Getty Images.

Scripture quotations marked NIV are taken from the Holy Bible, New International Version®. NIV®. Copyright © 1973, 1978, 1984 by International Bible Society. Used by permission of Zondervan. All rights reserved. [Biblica]

Scripture quotations marked GNT are taken from the Good News Translation — Second Edition. Copyright © 1992 by American Bible Society. Used by permission. All rights reserved.

Scripture quotations marked MSG are taken from THE MESSAGE. Copyright © 1993, 1994, 1995, 1996, 2000, 2001, 2002, 2003 by Eugene H. Peterson. Used by permission of NavPress Publishing Group. Website.

This book is printed on acid-free paper.

Because of the dynamic nature of the Internet, any web addresses or links contained in this book may have changed since publication and may no longer be valid. The views expressed in this work are solely those of the author and do not necessarily reflect the views of the publisher, and the publisher hereby disclaims any responsibility for them.

Dedicated to my parents; former and current members of St. George's Anglican Church, Nevis; St. George's Anglican Church, Antigua; St. David's Episcopal Church, Cambria Heights, New York; and the seminarians at Codrington College, Barbados.

CONTENTS

Acknowledgments ix
Foreword xi
Introduction xiii

Chapter 1 A Presumptuous Hope 1
Chapter 2 The Sacred Journey 18
Chapter 3 Thrown into the Deep End of the Pool 26
Chapter 4 Living on the Edge 39
Chapter 5 Do Not Quit; Get Fit 57
Chapter 6 On the Cutting Edge 74
Chapter 7 Coworkers with God 89
Chapter 8 Nurturing 120
Chapter 9 Reach and Touch 142

Appendix 169
About the Author 177

ACKNOWLEDGMENTS

First, I am indeed grateful to the Rev. Canon Dr. Cicely Broderick, Dr. Betty Carrington, and Mr. Euclid Jordan for encouraging me to tell my story.

I am also indebted to the Lilly Foundation for its grant, which allowed me some time off to travel, reflect, and write.

I could not have done this without the support of St. David's Parish. For the past thirty-four years, we have been together and have accomplished much. Thank you.

My gratitude goes out to my typists: Aaliyah Fernandez, Phyllis Fibleuil, Dorothy Lundy, Deana Nisbett, Jason Nisbett, Jereme Nisbett, and Jevon Nisbett.

Special thanks to Noella Jackman for her faithful, untiring effort at the computer in assisting me to produce this manuscript. Thank you so much.

Many thanks to Lynette Davson, Maxeen Gooden, Euclid Jordan, and Aletta Seales for your skills in proofreading.

Sincere thanks to Lorna Moodie-Jones for sharing her message. Thanks also to Oswald Green, my graphic artist.

I thank the Rt. Reverend Theodore Daniels for his editorial skill which enabled me to perfect this manuscript. Thank you also for the Foreword you kindly wrote. You are truly a servant of God.

Finally, my loving appreciation is expressed to my wife, Enid, for her support, patience, and understanding during this period of reflection and writing.

FOREWORD

This amazing book chronicles Dean Joshua Mastine Nisbett's life of dedicated service; one of his congregations spanned more than thirty-four years. He explains some of the challenges he faced and overcame as a Caribbean-born native who was called to ministry in a foreign land and learn to sing the Lord's song there. There were many challenges: no adequate place for his young family and him to live, not enough money to build a sanctuary for worship, the cosmopolitan mix of the fledgling congregation, and no documented history of the community where the congregation was called to carry out its communal ministry.

Nisbett met these challenges by calling upon his faith and trust in God, as he found solace in many scriptures from the Christian Bible, including passages mentioning his name, Joshua. The tenacity with which he and his family embraced the challenges is short of miraculous. Needless to say, he admits about times of sharing, despairing, and near abandonment. However, he was not one to give up on God, who called him to this ministry. He embraced the calling with resolve and boldly proclaimed God's Word to the congregation. The inspired congregation rose to their collective ministry and responded in word and deed.

Nisbett takes us back to the beginning of his call to ministry through to retirement (he ended his ministry at St. David's Episcopal Church, Cambria Heights, New York). He concludes that God is always faithful in promise to be with those chosen and called, even when difficult moments are not readily understood by us.

I commend the book, a marvelous reading of the story of a faithful priest who increasingly found his voice as a pastor, poet, and author called into ministry.

+The Rt. Rev. Dr. Theodore A. Daniels

Retired Episcopal Bishop

INTRODUCTION

Just before the day's second service, on May 7, 2017, the Reverend Canon Cecily Broderick and I were discussing plans for retirement. She said that I had a long and fruitful tenure at St. David's. Under my leadership, the congregation built a new house of worship, and there is a thriving congregation with a strong outreach ministry. She added that she could well imagine the many personal conflicts I had to resolve to maintain peace and harmony as the congregation continued to grow.

"This is a gift," she said. Mother Broderick also commented on our multimedia ministry with the current live streaming of the Sunday services. "You have prepared the congregation for the twenty-first century. You have a story to tell. There are not many long, effective pastorates these days. You should consider sharing your gifts through teaching and writing."

Mother Broderick was guided by the Holy Spirit that morning. She prompted me to do some soul searching, which became my personal intention as I presided at the Eucharist that morning. The Holy Spirit was truly at work, for there was an immediate response. At the end of the fellowship hour, I was happy to inform Mother Broderick that I decided to write on the topic, "Bloom Where You Are Planted."

Ironically, prior to that Sunday morning, I had a long process of discernment. For quite some time, I felt I was called to write my second book, but I kept changing the topic. What is so strange, the very morning I had the encounter with Mother Broderick, I wrote the first paragraph of an introduction to a book, *Recognizing God in Conflicts*. The genesis of this topic was in my earlier writing, *A Journey to the Promised Land*, where I wrote about the early history of Cambria Heights. The community is currently undergoing some stressful demographic changes that have caused much conflict, and I felt the urge to write about it. A few hours after I wrote that opening paragraph, I had the conversation with Mother Broderick, which changed the whole landscape. Is not this the way God's spirit often works, pointing us in new directions? Job reminds us, "It is God who directs the lives of his creatures, and everyone's life is in his power" (Job 12:10 TED). The prophet Isaiah says, "For my thoughts are not your thoughts, neither are your ways my ways" (Isaiah 55:8 NIV).

Mother Broderick's nudging was echoed two days later by Dr. Betty Carrington, a member of the congregation. As if that was not enough, it was further endorsed by another parishioner, Euclid "Cy" Jordan two days later. Over the next week, on three different occasions, I heard the same message from three persons. How can one ignore such promptings of the Holy Spirit? It is said, God often reveals part of the picture to one person and another part to another person; it is prudent to consult one another to discern God's counsel, guidance, and direction.

As I began writing on the theme "Bloom Where You Are Planted," I became aware of the fact that a few others have already written on the topic. I recalled the three individuals who prompted me to write about my experience. I also remembered Mary, the mother of our Lord, who said to the servants at the wedding feast in Cana, "Whatsoever he says unto you, do it" (John 2:5).

Initially, I thought the individuals had observed a thriving ministry at St. David's and were encouraging me to write about it. On further reflection, I thought they were messengers of God, like the prophets in ancient times who often introduced their message, "Thus, said the Lord." In that context, the full text of the message reads: "Thus, saith the Lord, wherever God has planted you God expects you to bloom." The challenge, then, was for me to bear witness to all that God has done in and through me. Accepting the challenge, I prayed that the Holy Spirit may bring all things to my remembrance and give me clarity of thought.

"Lord speak to me," I prayed, "that I may speak,

> Oh, use me Lord, use even me
> Just as you will, and when and where

Until at last your face I see,
Your rest, your joy your glory share."

While many scholars have written extensively on pastoral longevity, my approach will be a combination of theory and practical. Having served as an ordained priest in two parishes, the first for ten years and the latter for thirty-four years, longevity is obviously present. Thom S. Rainer in his little but profound book, *Autopsy of a Deceased Church*, noted the decrease in pastoral tenure. He observed that some pastors adopted a closed-door policy. No outreach programs into the community. He said such pastors often functioned more like a caretaker to its members. I am happy yet humbled to say that St. David's is not one of those congregations. When the caretaker pastor retires, the church closes its door, but I am praying that would not be our experience.

The question is, how did St. David's get on that "Exceptional" list? This narrative, I hope, will answer that question, which is honoring our baptismal covenant, discerning God's purpose in our lives, emptying and refilling of oneself, treading water, living on the edge, managing disappointments, trusting radically, mutual ministry, visioneering, outreach, and creative ministry.

While we must be careful not to over-spiritualize and over-rationalize things, we nevertheless need to have listening hearts to discern God's call in our daily lives. I am extremely grateful for the new direction in my writing. Indeed, it has enabled me to do some introspection, taking a serious in-depth review of my life, which is like looking in a car's rearview mirror. I reflected on my past journey: the places I have been, the obstacles I have overcome, and the progress I have made. In the midst of this reflection I hear a voice: "I have carried you since you were born; I have taken care of you from your birth" (Isaiah 46:3). With that reassurance, I shifted my vision from the rear to the front. Looking into the distance, I wondered how I was going to overcome the challenges, rejections, disappointments, and such like blazing at me? Then comes the voice of God once more: "Even when you are old, I will be the same. Even when your hair is turned gray, I will take care of you. I made you and will take care of you" (Isaiah 46:4).

John H. Sammis, in the hymn, *Trust and Obey*, wrote:

> When we walk with the Lord
> in the light of his word,
> what a glory he sheds on the way!
> While we do his good will,
> he abides with us still,
> and with all who will trust and obey.

The psalmist reminds us that our strength comes from the Lord, the maker of heaven and earth (Psalm 121). Walking with our Lord requires a radical trust in God. Relying on God's strength, not our own, taking calculated risks on an adventure with God. As you progress on the journey, looking back, you will begin to comprehend the journey. It is like Peter walking on the water with our Lord.

Henry Alford, the hymn writer, says: "We walk by faith, and not by sight."

Reflecting on my entire life, which of course includes my long tenure at St. David's, is not about me but about the Creator working through me (and others) to accomplish God's purpose. This has been a revealing exercise. Things that were once unclear have been clarified. God's revelation is manifested all around us, and we need to turn aside, like Moses, to observe our burning bush. Moses was intrigued by the burning bush. He advanced toward its mystery and discovered God's purpose in his life (Exodus 1:3). I think I can say I have been led to discern God's purpose in my life and have discovered my true self in the process.

Additionally, I have attempted to live out the true meaning of my names: Joshua Mastine Samuel. I have been able to connect my stories with God's story. This is not really my story; it is God's story. This reflection has helped me to identify with numerous biblical characters. The narrative is very personal. It is like me sharing my photo album with you. My hope is that it may serve as a mirror for you to look into and see yourself more clearly. It requires both biblical knowledge and wisdom, the wisdom to apply your life situation to the biblical narrative. In doing so, you will make these stories more relevant in your life. I hope you will be motivated to share your album with others.

Clarence and Alice Nisbett's wedding ceremony June 22, 1944

The Nisbett's family.

CHAPTER 1

A PRESUMPTUOUS HOPE

> Blessed is the man who trusts in me, God, the woman who sticks with God. They are like trees replanted in Eden, putting down roots near the rivers. Never a worry through the hottest of summer, never dropping a leaf, serene and calm through the droughts, bearing fresh fruit every season.
> —Jeremiah 17:7–8 The Message.

After graduating from school, I began working in the agricultural department in my home country, Nevis. My headmaster, Mr. Cedric Harper, had referred me to Mr. Ingle Blackett, an officer in that department. Arrangements were made for Mr. Blackett to pick me up at the Gingerland Senior School and take me to Prospect Estate, about four miles away. There, I was to learn the skill of grafting and budding fruit trees.

The very first day I was to report to the estate, I was ill. I was down with the mumps, high fever, muscle ache, and headache. I had no appetite and no energy. In addition to the physical discomfort, I was frustrated and disappointed in missing my first day at work. I thought, *Why now? I cannot even go out because of the contagiousness of the disease.*

Back in those days, there were no cell phones, and land lines were scarce. There was no instant way of communicating with the agricultural officer about my illness. This hurt just as much as the physical pain. The last thing I wanted was for the officer to believe that I was irresponsible and unreliable. That could cause me to lose my opportunity of employment.

A week later, Mr. Blackett was due to pick me up once more at the school. His Jeep was not there when I arrived. *I am early,* I thought, but then I was told it had just left.

What? Not again! I thought. *I can't afford to miss another appointment.*

I was annoyed with myself, but I later learned that the driver came very early because of his busy schedule. It was not my fault.

What difference does it make? I missed my ride.

Public transportation was limited and unreliable.

What must I do? I must get to Prospect as fast as I can.

I got into my "car," which I called "CN2." CN stands for "St. Christopher and Nevis," which was inscribed on the license plates of private automobiles in our country. Number 2 stood for my two feet.

Soon I was chasing the Jeep. I was a good sprinter in those days and had won many prizes. Long distance, I was only mediocre. The folks who saw me running that morning, not seeing who or what I was chasing—or who or what was chasing me—must have thought I was crazy.

I didn't care.

Fortunately for me, the route to the estate was downhill, and I made it in good time.

"How did you get here?" Mr. Blackett asked.

Pointing to my feet, I said, "CN2."

He smiled and hugged me. I had redeemed myself. Seeing a standpipe not far away, I reached for it and quenched my thirst.

The day went well. I was taught how to graft mango and avocado trees. I also learned about the budding of citrus trees. I was desperate to grasp the principle. Having missed the first class, I was playing catchup.

The ride back home was surely welcome to my exhausted, aching body. I told my parents how I ran from the Gingerland to Prospect.

"You did what? You must be crazy."

"No, I am not crazy. I just did what I had to do."

"How long did it take you?"

"How would I know? I don't have a watch."

"You must be really tired."

"You bet I am."

I reached for my bed, where I spent the next four days. My worst fear had come to pass: a relapse of the mumps. There was no end to the gargling with salt water, drinking of many fluids, and using all the local remedies that my mother concocted.

Finally, the mumps abated, and I was well enough to report to the estate the following week.

After my second orientation, I was officially employed, working two days per week at $2.50 per day. I went around the community, grafting and budding fruit trees. I kept a diary, which was examined periodically by my supervisor, who increased my days because of the demand.

Some months later, I was promoted and appointed to a permanent position in the forestry department. I was there for a while, before being transferred to Prospect Estate as the foreman. The untimely and tragic drowning of my predecessor, Lewis, created a vacancy. Lewis was scheduled to travel to St. Augustine, Trinidad, to study agriculture. The question was, "Who will fill that void?"

One day, while I was in the experimental shed (where we keep the potted plants), I saw the superintendent of agriculture, Mr. Philip Evelyn, approaching. He was dressed in his usual short khaki trousers, long brown socks, and white shirt. After a formal exchange of greetings, he said, "Mr. Nisbett, the department is considering sending you to St. Augustine to further your studies in agriculture."

I was flabbergasted and excited. "Really?" I replied. "What an honor to be considered."

"Well, you have been with us for some time and have exhibited some fine characteristics. More than that, we observe you are eager to learn."

His words touched my inner being. A glow radiated on my face. Unfortunately, for lack of a mirror, I was not able to see it.

"So what do you think? Are you interested?"

I paused. He looked at me intently, wondering why I was hesitating "How soon do you need an answer?" I asked.

He looked at me even more keenly and said, "By the end of the week."

"Very well, sir. I'll have an answer by then."

As he left, I thought, *Mastine, what have you done? This is a chance of a lifetime. Have you blown it? Are you crazy?*

Shortly after my confirmation, I began serving as an altar boy. Later I became a chorister, Boy Scout, youth group leader, Sunday school teacher, vestry member, Eucharistic minister, and lay reader. By the time I was twenty-one, I had served in every area of lay ministry.

"Quite an impressive résumé," you would probably say, but it was not a guarantee against suffering and adversity, as I soon discovered.

When I was sixteen years old, a girl I had a crush on invited me to a beach picnic at Indian Castle in Nevis. It was hosted by the Methodist Youth Fellowship. Everyone was having a good time. In the late afternoon, I was caught in a quicksand. It was like a whirlpool. The current was pulling me farther and farther away from the shore. I desperately tried to swim in the opposite direction, but all my attempts were futile. I was panicking, crying for help, and taking in water at same time. Not far away was a young man whose last name was Ferguson. He advanced toward me. We struggled together. I remember praying a short prayer: "Lord, have mercy." Then I became unconscious. When I regained consciousness, I was on the beach, vomiting. I was surrounded by a crowd; an older lady was fanning me with a piece of paper. I could hear someone saying, "Don't crowd him. Give him some air."

The older lady gave me something to smell. I later learned it was smelling salts.

"You are a lucky young man," someone said, "You were practically dead. The Lord must have saved you for a special purpose. We had to give you CPR."

"Who gave me CPR?"

"The same old lady who was giving you the smelling salts."

Ironically, it was not the girl I had a crush on who saved me, but a toothless old lady. Nodding, in a weak voice, I thanked them all for saving my life. Looking around, I saw Ferguson. Nodding to him, in a low voice, I thanked him personally for saving my life.

I was shocked when he told me he was not the one who saved me. "I couldn't manage you, so I went ashore and sought help."

He pointed to another young man, Edric Williams, and said, "He was the one who saved you."

Edric, who was my neighbor, said, "When I found you, you were unconscious, and I just pushed you ashore like a log of wood."

I was so grateful to these two men and others for their acts of kindness, but more so for God's saving grace. Countless others have drowned at that beach, but I was saved.

That night, I was haunted by the words "You were unconscious, and I pushed you ashore like a log of wood. You were practically dead. The Lord must have saved you for a special purpose."

For several weeks, I had nightmares reliving that experience. I thought, *What did I do to deserve God's grace—this new lease on life?*

Grace, of course, is God's unconditional favor. We do not earn it, nor do we deserve it.

Before I had that near-death experience, I was already considering a vocational calling to the ordained ministry. That incident helped to clarify certain things. I was reminded of the story of Jonah, who was rescued from the belly of the whale so that he might adhere to God's commission to preach to the people of Nineveh. While God is not the author of evil or adversity, God allows this to happen and then speaks to us through the same adversity. Unfortunately, sometimes this is the only time God gets our undivided attention. However, we must be cautious of over-spiritualizing or over-rationalizing our circumstances. We can be deceived by our own reasoning. A careful, reasoned conclusion does not mean we have discerned God's call.

Hence the need to listen and discern what God is saying to us and not what we think or hope God is saying. It is amazing how God works, oftentimes turning the negative into a positive. Yes! God moves in mysterious ways, His wonders to perform. The Apostle Paul said, "Know that all things work together for the good, for those who love God, who are called according to his purpose" (Romans 8:28).

Note, the text says, "All things," not some things or most things, but all things. Note also the text does not say we "see all things work together for good." Just because we cannot see it, it does not mean God cannot see it.

Indeed, sometimes the evidence of the good is revealed long after us.

In the infinite wisdom of God, we were all created for a specific purpose. Our greatest pursuit should be discerning God's purpose in and for our lives.

Eleanor Roosevelt said, "What we are is God's gift to us. What we become is our gift to God."

I wrestled for a long while with the 'call' to the ordained ministry. I was born on September 10, 1946. Nineteen days later, on the Feast of St. Michael and All Angels, I was baptized. Nineteen days. Reflecting on it now, my parents, Clarence and Alice Nisbett, seemed rather anxious to have me baptized. Were they led by the Spirit to act with such immediacy? Or I wonder whether it was the priest, Father Ronald Thompson, our immediate neighbor, who encouraged my parents to have me baptized at such an early age. Was my health in jeopardy? In our culture, it was customary to keep newborn babies indoors for nine days before they were taken outside. This means, more than likely, that my first public appearance was at my baptism at St. George's Anglican Church, Nevis, on September 29, 1946. I am not certain whether any of my siblings were baptized that early. But as I think about it now, I likened my parents to Elkanah and Hannah in the Old Testament. They took Samuel, their newly born child, to Eli, the priest at the temple, and dedicated him for God's service. Father Thompson was the officiating priest at my baptism; strangely enough, I was baptized as Samuel Mastine. But I was not the first child of my parents, as was the case of Hannah. She was childless and promised God that she would dedicate the child to the Lord if God would bless her with a child. No; I was the sixth of my parents' children.

I was born into a very devoted Christian family; my maternal great-grandfather was a Sunday school superintendent. My maternal grandmother, Marie, was very saintly. Dressed usually in white, she not only attended Sunday mass, but the week day masses as well. Father Aldric Hassel, the priest then, often referred to her as St. Marie. My paternal grandfather was the sexton/lay reader for about forty years. He was succeeded by my father, who held that position for almost forty years, until his death.

Like the tree replanted in Eden that the prophet Jeremiah referred to in the quote at the beginning of this chapter, my ancestors were like a river, providing nourishment for my young and tender roots. Planted by the stream of waters, I was encouraged to bring forth fruits in due season. I was surrounded by a great cloud of witnesses who were either still participating in the race or who had finished it. They welcomed me into the race.

Bloom Wherever God Plants You

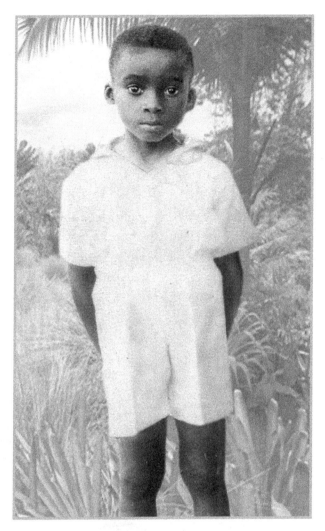

Mastine

As a child, I had a speech impediment, so my parents sent me to preschool to assist me in overcoming that deficiency. Moses, you may recall, complained to God that he was no orator when the Lord told him to go to Pharaoh and plead the case for the Israelites. In response, God appointed Aaron as the priest. It was all part of the divine plan. I was sent to preschool so I'd be equipped for the task ahead. And so, at age twelve, I was confirmed, taking full responsibility for my baptismal covenant. Fanny Cosby's hymn, *I Am Thine, O Lord*, seemed rather appropriate:

> Consecrate me now to thy service, Lord,
> by the power of grace divine.
> Let my soul look up with steadfast hope,
> and my will be lost in thine.
>
> Draw me nearer, nearer, blessed Lord,
> to the cross where thou hast died.
> Draw me nearer, nearer, nearer, blessed Lord,
> to thy precious bleeding side.

The critical moment came when my girlfriend and I broke up. I was about twenty-two years old. I felt devastated. St. Mark, the evangelist, records that Jesus only began his public ministry after the arrest of John the Baptist: "Now after John was arrested, Jesus came to Galilee, proclaiming the good news of God" (Mark 1:14).

St George's Anglican Church Nevis

John's crisis was the springboard for our Lord's public ministry. The Chinese view a crisis in two ways: a danger or an opportunity. There is much food for thought here. The break-up of my relationship was a critical moment when I totally surrendered to God's call. I remember going to Canon Blant and saying to him, "I am ready to test my vocation to the priesthood."

The afternoon after my conversation with Mr. Evelyn, my supervisor, I went for a walk in our backyard. Sitting under a mango tree, I poured out my soul to God: *Why are you making it so difficult for me? I am confused. Yes, I want to go to St. Augustine, but I can still feel a pull toward the priesthood. Lord, which route should I take?*

For a good moment, I sat there in silence, with tears streaming down my eyes. Blissful tears. Exhausted from my emotional journey, I fell asleep and dreamt I was nervously crossing a bridge; an old man came and helped me across. Soon after that, I was awakened when a ripe mango fell on me. I was surprised that I had fallen asleep under the tree, something I had never done before, yet it was a very restful sleep. I said to myself, *anyone who sees me sleeping here would think I am crazy.* I got up and ate the mango. It was delicious, although it was the sourest mango we had on the property. But I was hungry, having not eaten since breakfast.

Later that evening, my dad asked me, "Why were you sleeping under the mango tree?" I was taken by surprise. I did not know he had seen me.

"You have been sneaking up on me, Dad."

"No, I just want to know that you are all right."

"I'm fine. I am not crazy. At least, not yet."

"What do you mean by that?"

I told my parents my dilemma. Mom, at that time, had already had a stroke. Her speech was impaired, but there was a glow on her jolly face.

"Mom, which route should I take: St. Augustine to study agriculture?" She shook her head vehemently in disapproval.

"Should I go for the priesthood?"

She nodded her head in approval and blurted out the word, "Yes."

Her voice was clear and distinct. It was the first time in a long while that she spoke so clearly. I repeated the question three or four times, not because I did not understand her, but I realized it was therapeutic, as I was acting like a speech therapist.

I immediately recalled the story of Zechariah, the priest who became mute for nine months and only regained his speech when he was about to name his son John the Baptist.

"Okay, Mom. I heard you. Priest."

She uttered, "Yes."

I turned to my father and asked, "And what do you think, Dad?"

I knew he would encourage me to pursue the priesthood. Still, I wanted to hear him say it.

"Well, son, either way, you will serve God and the society. But, of course, you know we would be delighted if you choose the priesthood. Remember, though, one is a career; the other is a calling."

The next day, I met my priest, Canon Blant, and shared the news of the scholarship to study agriculture. He seemed excited but remained calm. He was an Englishman who rarely shared his emotions. I had already been interviewed by our bishop regarding my candidacy for seminary.

"You are very blessed," Canon Blant said.

"I guess so," I replied, "but now I am even more confused."

"Why are you confused?"

"I have a decision to make, and I don't know what to do."

"That's what discernment is all about."

"Yes, but it is not easy."

"Discipleship is not easy, either, but our Lord said, 'My yoke is easy and my burden is light.' Follow your instinct."

"Well, I guess that is what I have to do."

The following day, I went to see my supervisor in his office. I was still ambivalent about my future.

"Well, Mr. Nisbett," he said, "I trust you have an answer for me."

"I want to thank you for advocating on my behalf, but I have to decline the offer."

Mr. Evelyn's face dropped. He leaned back in his chair. I got even more nervous, my stomach churning over.

After a long pause, he said, "Mr. Nisbett, are you crazy? Do you know how many people would like this opportunity?"

"I can well imagine. But for some time now, I have been contemplating going to seminary to test my vocation for the ordained ministry."

He was Anglican like myself. He looked rather surprised; he perked up and said, "I knew you were involved in the church, but I had no idea you were contemplating the priesthood."

"Yes sir, and I am hoping to enter seminary in the fall."

"But I am offering you a scholarship, which you have declined, as you await something you are not sure about. Isn't that crazy?"

"I guess you can say so."

He wished me God's blessings and said, "You are giving up grafting fruit trees to graft souls. Not a bad idea. I guess I have to come to hear you preach, Father Nisbett."

"Let us not get ahead of ourselves."

"Good. But you won't hear my confessions, though."

"That's okay."

As I left Mr. Evelyn's office, I felt somewhat relieved. I had made a decision, but Satan was still busy; my doubts lingered on. My biggest fear was failure. Failure at St. Augustine was bad enough, but people do not readily forgive failure when it comes to God's work. They want you to be perfect.

In my mind, I could hear some folks saying, *So, who does Mastine think he is? Why didn't he stick to agriculture?*

Besides, the only other person from the parish who pursued theological training did not make it. True, there are two others on the island who pursued it; one died before he completed his training, and the other is still in seminary. Not much, as far as role models.

Was I a fool to decline the government's scholarship?

The thought haunted me for a few days. A bird in the hand is worth two in the bush. Going to work was not easy. I kept on wondering what my colleagues must be saying: "What a fool he must be to give up a government scholarship for something he was not even certain of." At times, I really felt like a fool. The clergy stipend was a meager pittance compared to what I was likely to earn as a government employee. With youth on my side, I could have continued my career with the government and later pursued the theological training.

What a fool am I? I thought. A radical decision, but is it a wise one? But this is what discernment is about?

Discernment comes from the Latin word *discerne*, which means "to separate, to distinguish, to determine, to sort out" (Suzanne G. Farnham et al., p. 23). It is possible to hear many voices in our lives. Voices from loved ones, peers, ego, careers and culture. These voices, while they may be good, may nevertheless, drown out the voice of God. The question is, how do we distinguish God's voice from that of others? Discernment may be understood as "apprehending" rather than "comprehending" (Farnham et al., 2002.p. 3). Discerning can be like driving a car at night. The headlights cast only enough light for us to see a short distance.

Ultimately, discernment requires our willingness to act in faith on our sense of what God wants us to do (Farnham et al., p. 23). That is radical trust.

Newman, in one of his hymns says:

> Lead, kindly light, amidst th' encircling gloom,
> lead thou me on!
> The night is dark, and I am far from home.
> Lead thou me on!
> Keep thou my feet, I do not ask to see
> the distant scene; one step enough for me.

We need to listen, to be attentive to God's voice, and then to act, knowing that God blesses even our mistakes (Farnham et al., p. 23). After much prayer and listening, the time came for me to formally resign from what seemed to be a promising career. Computers were not yet in existence, and my typing skills were limited. I had no choice but a good old-fashioned handwritten letter. Writing it was an emotional experience. Severing a relationship with people I had just bonded with. In my mind, I could still hear the tempter whispering, *Are you sure you know what you are doing? Risking everything.*

I made a giant step and submitted my resignation.

"I am no prophet, nor a prophet's son; but I am a herdsman, and a dresser of sycamore trees and the Lord took me from following the flock, and the Lord said to me, "Go prophesy to my people Israel" (Amos 7:14–15). Like Amos, I was a dresser of trees (not sycamore trees, but I grafted many fruit trees). And now after forty years, I can still return home, and someone can offer me a Julie mango from a tree I grafted.

Simon Peter, Andrew, his brother, and James and John, sons of Zebedee, were called away from their fishing nets to be fishers of men. In like manner, I was called from the grafting of fruit trees to allowing God to use me in the grafting of hearts of human beings. The Collect for Proper 17 of the Book of Common Prayer (BCP) reads thus:

Lord of all power and might, who art the author and giver of all good things, graft in our hearts the love of thy name, increase in us true religion, nourish us with all goodness, and bring forth in us the fruit of good works, through Jesus Christ our Lord.

In baptism, we are adopted into God's covenant family: The Father, the Son, and the Holy Spirit. It is like grafting. We are the rootstock created in God's image and therefore capable of producing ordinary fruit, but if we are to produce the hybrid fruit of love, forgiveness, kindness, gentleness, and long suffering, we need to be grafted into the true vine, so that we the branches may bear good fruit. At my baptism, I was grafted and adopted into God's family. Subsequently, God called me to assist in grafting others into the Body of Christ. In St. John's Gospel, Jesus told his disciples, "You did not choose me but I chose you."

For some time now, whenever anyone asks me why I chose the priesthood, I respond in saying, "I didn't choose it. Rather, it chose me."

This conviction came in hindsight after much reflection and revelation, which I shall write about later. However, what if I had stayed in the agricultural field? I think I would have continued to serve God, but in a different way. Perhaps I would not have fulfilled God's purpose in my life. That is what makes discernment so challenging. The Honorable Vance Amory (former premier of Nevis) and I started the lay reader ministry together. At that time, Amory resided with Canon Edgar Blant, our rector. Many thought he had a vocation for the ordained ministry. As it turned out, he did not. Nevertheless, he ministered to the citizens of St. Kitts and Nevis in a very special way. Perhaps that was God's purpose for his life. Sir Hugh Rawlins, former chief justice of the Eastern Caribbean Supreme Court, and I were neighbors in our formative years. Currently, he is an administrative judge in Geneva, Switzerland. He too bloomed where he was planted. God calls each of us. There are variety of calls, and no call is inherently better or higher than any other. It is our faithfulness to God and not our station in life that honors a call (Farnham et al., p. 23).

The time came for me to venture out, like Peter. I left my comfort zone and took my first baby steps with our Lord. Leaving your comfort zone and taking such bold risks in faith is just like walking on water. That is a radical trust, a presumptuous hope. In my Confirmation class, I was taught that one should always approach the sacrament of Holy Communion reverently and with much humility. I had to memorize the prayer of Humble Access:

> We do not presume to come to this thy Table,
> o merciful Lord, trusting in our own righteousness
> but in thy manifold and great mercies.
> We are not worthy so much as to gather up
> the crumbs under thy table.
> But thou art the same Lord, whose property is always to
> have mercy.
> Grant us, therefore, gracious Lord, so to eat the flesh of
> thy dear
> Son Jesus Christ
> and drink his blood, that we may continually
> dwell in him and he in us. (BCP, p. 337)

If one is required to approach the sacrament with such reverence and respect, then one ought to approach the sacred vocation with similar humility. To that end, I paraphrased this prayer as I contemplated the ordained ministry:

> I do not presume to come to this sacred vocation
> trusting in my own righteousness.
> I am not worthy to baptize anyone, because
> only you can baptize, and it is in your name that
> we are baptized.
> I am not worthy to gather the crumbs under your table,
> much
> more to preside at your table.

> I am not worthy to proclaim your word,
> because I lack the wisdom, and I am no orator.
> I am not worthy to pronounce the absolution to the
> penitent, being a sinner myself.
> But you are the same Lord, whose property is always
> to have mercy.
> Grant me, therefore, gracious Lord, so to join you in
> the sacred ministry of your church.
> Amen.

Like Amos, I gave up the dressing of trees in pursuit of the dressing of souls. Presumptuous hope. A hope that is built on Christ, the solid rock. Edward Mote puts it very nicely in these wonderful words:

> My hope is built on nothing less
> than Jesus Christ, my righteousness.
> I dare not trust the sweetest frame,
> but wholly lean on Jesus's name.
> On Christ, the solid rock I stand,
> all other ground is sinking sand. (Levas. 99)

On that late September day, I left my parents' home in Nevis on a journey to the United Theological College of the West Indies in Jamaica. What a parting that was. Even now, as I write about it, I get emotional and tearful. I did not know I could touch those feelings after forty-six years. They are fresh and raw, as if it were yesterday. This is perhaps the most painful exercise I have had in recent times. Enid, my wife, looked at me and saw I was overwhelmed, all choked up. I felt like I had a boulder in my throat.

"If something is so painful, why do you go there?" she asked.

After taking a few days' break from writing, I returned to the manuscript and recalled my mother, whose speech and mobility were affected by the stroke, saying to me, "I'll be praying for you."

The prayer of a devoted mother never goes unanswered. I remember those mothers who, when they can no longer hold you in their arms, would say they hold you in their prayers.

Reflecting on it now, I wonder if when my mother uttered the words that she would be praying for me, did she remember the day she took me to the church and had me baptized? I wonder what she thought then. Did she ever perceive herself as Hannah when she had me baptized as Samuel, even before she weaned me? Did she ever think I would become a priest? Now one week short of my baptism's twenty-fifth anniversary, she said goodbye to me as I left for seminary to study for the priesthood. A presumptuous hope, a dream she would not witness in the flesh, as she died five months later. Is not this the way life often is? We have our specific assignment in God's comprehensive plan. Once we have completed that task, we make our exit.

While my mother said goodbye, my father embraced me. The embrace was stronger than words, for in that hug, as I understand it now, there were not only the two of us, but his father, Joshua (my grandfather), St. Marie, my grandmother, and all those faithful people who had served the church for centuries and had looked to the dawn of this new day. Phillip Brooks, in the well-known Christmas carol *O Little Town of Bethlehem*, writing about the joy of the advent of the Messiah, which for generations was long expected, says

> The hopes and fears of all the years
> are met in thee tonight.

As my father and I embraced, he spoke, yet not with much words, but with that powerful embrace, he said, "Son, the hopes and aspirations of all the years are met in you, this day."

A presumptuous hope.

Bloom Wherever God Plants You

Mastine

CHAPTER 2

THE SACRED JOURNEY

As I said goodbye to my parents, nuclear family, extended family, and church family, I could feel the support of the community, but I also felt a burden that all eyes were fixed on me, and I dared not let them down.

In hindsight, it was not just they who were looking on, but my ancestors as well. Most importantly, God was looking on because this was all part of God's providential plan. While this may seem intimidating, it need not be because I was dealing with a loving, caring, forgiving, and generous God. Scripture tells us there is no fear in love, but perfect love drives out fear (1 John 4:18). God invites us to walk on water, taking risks and even making mistakes. What is more, God acknowledges our faithfulness and blesses us, in spite of our mistakes. Abraham was an adulterer, Jacob was a conniver and deceiver, Moses was a murderer, David was an adulterer and murderer, Rahab was a prostitute, yet God used them despite their shortcomings. It was obvious that the journey I was about to begin was no ordinary trip. It was a sacred journey. Like Abraham, I began an adventure with God. Like the psalmist, I said, "I lift up mine eyes to the hills, from where my help will come. My help comes from the Lord, who made heaven and earth" (Psalm 121:1).

I recalled Mr. and Mrs. Clarence Dore giving me a card with a monetary gift when I left for seminary. (I had grafted many fruit trees for the Dores.) The pink card was one of Helen Keller's production, with the

Bloom Wherever God Plants You

words "Climb til Your Dreams Come Through." It was an inspirational card, which I kept on my desk throughout my four years in seminary. It became my personal mission statement and my driving force.

Entering those sacred walls of the United Theological College of the West Indies, I learned two things: humility and self-control. I arrived at the college one day late; I was reprimanded, not so much by the administration but by the student association.

"How dare you enter these sacred grounds a day late?" asked the president. "Have you no respect for this institution?"

Shocked, humiliated, and almost trembling, I replied:

"I am sorry, but it was the earliest flight from the eastern Caribbean to Jamaica."

"Then we should have been informed."

"My humble apologies, sir."

"Now will you introduce yourself to this distinguished body?"

"My name is Mastine Nisbett."

"Stop. Stand on the chair."

I complied by standing on the chair. I was wearing a pair of sandals.

"How dare you enter the cafeteria with your tentacles exposed? Don't you dare do that again. Now proceed to introduce yourself."

"My name is Mastine Nisbett."

There was a tumultuous interruption.

"What did you say?" they chanted.

I was beginning to feel many emotions within me. Once again, I introduced myself.

"My name is Mastine Nisbett."

The interruption grew louder, and I was getting annoyed and nervous. Then the president said,

"Let me ask you for the third time, what exactly is your name?"

By this time, I was wondering whether I had come to the right place. I tried hard to exercise some self-control. I did not want them to get under my skin. I decided to state my full name and said,

"My name is Joshua Mastine Samuel Nisbett."

Someone shouted,

"But the grub is confused. First it said its name is Mastine Nisbett, now it is saying its name is Joshua Mastine Samuel Nisbett. Which one are we supposed to believe?"

The president said, "Evidently, you don't understand. You are a Grub. You are nothing, so from henceforth you shall say 'its' instead of 'my.' Do you understand that, Grub?"

Reluctantly, and with much internal anger, I grumbled, "Yes."

The president then said, "Now let the grub introduce itself properly to this renowned illustrious body."

Under my breath, I said, "Illustrious? This is crazy. It is ridiculous."

Summing up all the courage I could find within me, I nervously said, "Its name is Joshua Mastine Samuel Nisbett."

There was loud applause, as the entire body rose from their seats and welcomed me into their body. I was then asked to read aloud the following psalm:

> Lord I am not high minded. I have no proud looks. I do not exercise myself in great matters which are too high for me, but I refrain my soul and keep it low like as a child that is weaned from his mother, yea my soul is even as a weaned child that is within me. (Psalm 131)

It was one of the most humiliating experiences I ever endured. My ego was shot. Any slight accomplishment can cause a surge of the ego, like that of an adrenaline rush. Acceptance into the seminary certainly had a competitive edge over St. Augustine. Besides, indigenous priests were just coming to the horizon. For over three hundred years, all the priests who served in my home parish were expatriates.

I could have easily thought I had arrived and celebrate my accomplishment over and against the nay-sayers, who thought I was foolish to decline the government scholarship. I could have easily gotten ahead of myself and elevated myself on a pedestal, setting my ego up for the inevitable fall, for a haughty spirit precedes a fall.

The initiation, which seemed cruel at the time, was nevertheless designed to make me humble. Two of my classmates had their egos similarly crushed on their arrival. One was a former principal of a school, and the other, the CEO of a large firm. They both arrived with much prestige and a chip on their shoulder. They found themselves in a subordinate position and were forced to take orders from people much younger than themselves. They were not happy campers.

The journey required the emptying of oneself. The Apostle Paul, writing to the Philippians, said "Let this mind be in you, which was also in Christ Jesus, who being in the form of God, thought it not robbery to be equal with God. But made himself of no reputation, and took upon him the form of a servant, and was made in the likeness of men and being found of a servant, he emptied himself, and became obedient unto death, even death on the cross" (Philippians 2:5–8).

It is noteworthy that this passage of scripture is usually read on Palm Sunday. It speaks about Christ "emptying" himself, the deity, the Creator, becoming a creature, the master becoming a slave, a servant to redeem humanity. My sacred journey began when I decided to follow Christ, turning away from a promising career and, at the same time, subjecting myself to much humiliation. This journey is a marathon, not a sprint.

Evelyn Atwater Cummins, in her hymn, writes:

> I know not where the road will lead
> I follow day by day
> or where it ends; I only know
> I walk the king's highway.
>
> I know not if the road is long,
> and no one else can say,
> but rough or smooth, uphill or down,
> I walk the king's highway.
> (Hymnal 1982, 647)

As I traveled on the road of that sacred journey, I am more convinced I did not choose God, but God chose me for this purpose (John 15:16).

I also heard those famous words of our Lord: "I am the way, the truth, and the life" (John 14:6). It was a transforming journey, radicalizing my Sunday school theology and changing my spiritual diet from milk to solid food, as the Apostle Paul suggests *(1 Corinthians 3:2)*.

My first year in seminary was quite challenging. I was home sick. I struggled with my classes, particularly Greek and Hebrew. In addition, I had the disadvantage of being out of school for almost ten years. There were times when I wondered "did I make the right decision? Was I foolish to pursue the priesthood? Am I a misfit? Maybe St. Augustine is where I really belong." The card on my desk kept on reminding me 'Climb til your Dreams come Through.' That I tried, but then my mother passed during the second semester. It was a good thing I had returned home for Christmas and saw her alive for the last time. We joked about going to St. Augustine or seminary. It was very evident that she was happy with the choice I had made.

At her funeral, I officiated at the concluding service at the grave side because Canon Blant had to leave for another service. Yes, it was emotional. It was special. It was a privilege and an honor to conduct my first committal and that of my mother. After the casket was lowered, a grasshopper perched on the shoulder of my white surplice. I brushed it away, but it returned. I decided to allow it to remain. During the singing of a hymn and before the closing of the grave, I looked at the lowered casket, and saw something like an image of my mother, waving her hand saying:

"Don't cry, everything is going to be alright."

With that, all my tears were dried, and the service concluded without a hitch. Obviously, there was a void caused by my mother's demise. There was no grief counseling. Life must go on. Back to seminary, to struggle with the books and classes. When I felt down, discouraged, or foolish to have chosen seminary in lieu of St. Augustine, I simply read my mission statement:

'Climb Til your Dreams come Through.' Yes, and there were times when I felt the presence of my mother whispering those words, priesthood not St. Augustine.

Inasmuch as I had returned to seminary shortly after the burial of my mother, I was anxiously looking forward to spending my first summer vacation at home. However, Bishop Lindsay had other plans. In late spring I was informed that I was selected to be the Assistant Chaplain at Camp Medley, in our newly formed companion Diocese of Fredrickton, New Brunswick, Canada. I am disappointed in not returning home for the summer, but I am excited in going to Camp Medley. I was equally delighted, when our companion diocese expressed much confidence in me and requested that I return the following summer as chaplain of the camp. My third summer is even more exciting. Selected as the theological student representative for the Anglican North America and Caribbean Conference, ANACC in Tobago.

At the conclusion of the conference, I traveled to Antigua, where I was ordained deacon on St. Peter and Paul Day, June 29, 1974, at St. John's Cathedral.

At the ordination service, while kneeling, during the hymn, "*Veni Creator Spiritus*" (Come Holy Ghost, our souls inspire,) I felt the presence of my mother and was overwhelmed with tears. I knew she was rejoicing with me that day.

I stayed in Antigua for a month doing some research on the Antigua Grammar School. On Sundays, I assisted the Rev. Stephen Eardley at St. Philip's and St. George's parishes. After my sojourn in Antigua, I spent a month in my home country. This was my first extended stay since entering seminary. Canon Blant was on long leave, and I was given the spiritual oversight of my home parish. What an honor and a privilege. The dream was partially fulfilled. The reception was warm and much rejoicing, with a son of the soil advancing to such a milestone. My visit to my former workplace was equally jubilant, and I returned, energized, to seminary for my final year. I had taken a giant leap of faith, and I was on my last lap approaching the finishing line.

Returning to seminary as Deacon Nisbett, I was elected president of the Anglican Student Association and immediately recalled my last year in high school. I then had the privilege of being the head prefect and the school's first valedictorian. As deacon, I assisted at the Church of the Ascension in Mona Heights, Jamaica.

Being human, these new assignments certainly boosted my ego. I remembered how I had disliked being treated as a grub in my first year, so I tried to keep my ego from being too inflated. Then came the elevation to the priesthood in my home parish on St. James Day, July 25, 1975. A historical day in the parish, and the entire island of Nevis. The first ordination service in my home parish. The presumptuous hope!

A service witnessed not only by those physically present, but also my deceased mother and my ancestors for as the preface before Sanctus says:

"Therefore, with angels and archangels, and with all the company of heaven, we laud and magnify thy glorious name, evermore praising and singing …" Were my deceased mother and my ancestors present too?

What is more, at that ordination service Allister Rawlins received and answered the call to the ordained ministry. It is also worth noting that earlier in Allister's life I taught him in Sunday school and taught him how to graft fruit trees. Now I have helped to usher him into the ordained ministry.

A presumptuous hope.

The Eric Joseph, the Rev. J. Mastine Nisbett, the Rt. Rev. Orland Lindsay, the Rev. Wilfred Daniel, and the Rev. St. Clair Williams, ordination to the diaconate June 29, 1974.

Bloom Wherever God Plants You

The Rev. J. Mastine Nisbett June 29, 1974

CHAPTER 3

THROWN INTO THE DEEP END OF THE POOL

St George's Anglican Church Nevis

When some swimming instructors or parents teach young children to swim, they take them to the deep end of the pool, release them, and tell them to swim to the other end of the pool. Scary, isn't it? That is not a good introduction to swimming, you probably say. But that is exactly how I felt when introduced into the parish life as a priest.

Normally, newly ordained priests are appointed as a curate in a parish and be supervised by a senior clergy for one to three years before their first appointment as a parish priest.

On August 1, 1975, after my ordination to the priesthood, I was appointed priest in charge of St. George's Parish, Antigua. I was thrown into the deep end of the pool with little supervision, except for a brief six-month oversight by Dean Pestaina, the dean of St. John's Cathedral.

After my apprenticeship as priest in charge was over, I was appointed parish priest of the said parish.

Now, a priest in charge is like an engagement; being a parish priest is like the marriage.

I wondered if I was that gifted to be placed on such a fast track.

There were four hundred people on the parish register, certainly not a small parish. Some questioned the wisdom of Bishop Lindsay for appointing a rookie priest to such an established parish.

"What a foolish thing to do," the critics said. "Absolutely absurd and ridiculous; no respect for the parish. He should have been sent to Barbuda,"

Like a young soldier, I was placed on the firing line, or like a receptionist who gets all the complaints and insults.

The rejection was not only parochial but also felt from a few lay popes at the cathedral. They claimed to have some expertise in grooming young priests. They also thought it was unwise to send me out on my own in the parish. When it was announced that I was coming to the cathedral as part of a pulpit exchange, a lay pope said to me,

"I heard you are coming to the cathedral; you had better be good."

I rebutted, "Would you have said that to a white priest?"

Paralyzed silence.

On another occasion, the dean of the cathedral invited me to do a three-hour meditation on Good Friday. One individual said to me,

"I am not going to sit in my usual seat in the choir stall. I am going to sit in the gallery, and I'm taking a book with me to read, just in case I am bored."

I said to her, "Come and see."

I did not preach on the traditional seven last words from the cross, although I cannot recall the theme I used. However, at the end of the service, the lady congratulated me, saying, "I did not open the book, and I could have listened to you for another hour." She was not the only person with congratulatory messages. Bishop Lindsay remarked that he heard portions of the meditation, which was broadcast live on a local radio station. He too said it was good.

What did I do with all these complaints and insults? There were two options: I could absorb them like a sponge and soak them up. That, of course, would be foolish and detrimental to my health. The second option was to filter them like the kidneys eliminate waste. This was the most prudent thing to do. As a bachelor, I had ample time for reflection.

I asked myself these questions: What motivated the bishop to express such confidence in me? Was it my involvement in lay ministry? Was it my work experience prior to seminary? Was it a report from my warden at seminary? Was it the recommendation of the Commission on Ministry? Was it my chaplaincy at Camp Medley? Was it my leadership as president of the Anglican Student Association? Was it my involvement in the ANAC Conference in Tobago? Was it my ministerial work in the parishes subsequent to my ordination to the diaconate? Was it the guidance of the Holy Spirit? Was it sheer foolishness? Or all the above?

Reflecting on those questions, the word *foolishness* continued to stand out. If the bishop was a fool to appoint me as the parish priest, then I, his representative, could easily be considered a fool as well. How could I convince the critics otherwise? In college, I was indoctrinated as a grub, a worm, and had to memorize Psalm 131, the Psalm of Humility; this made me feel like a fool.

Initially, I was overwhelmed and had a few outbursts in the parish. Sensing some rejection, I threatened the congregation one morning, saying, "My suitcases are still packed, and my barrels have not yet arrived."

I felt foolish afterwards, as I recalled my homiletics professor saying, "Whenever you step into the pulpit, always remember the words, 'Sir, we would see Jesus.' While some may very well be there to see you, your task as the preacher is to show them Jesus."

Did I show them Jesus that morning? I leave that for you, the reader, to decide. What I do know is, I showed them my frustration and my humanness.

Did it work? Well, I subsequently spent ten productive years in the parish. Was my threat a contributing factor to my tenure? I leave that for the congregation to decide.

My second outburst was when someone said to me, "You could be my son." I retorted, "Yes, but I am not, and I am your priest."

She grumbled something under her breath and walked away. A month later, I ministered to her while she was hospitalized for a fortnight. Remorseful, she apologized for her previous behavior and commented that no one had cared for her the way I did.

My third outburst resulted from an ongoing challenge we were experiencing in the parish. Several times, I brought it to the attention of Mr. Isaac, the rector's warden, who had the authority to resolve the issue. The problem continued. One Sunday morning, on my arrival at the church, I felt frustrated and spiritually impoverished. Turning to the warden, I said, "Mr. Isaac, I would like you to deliver the message this morning. I am not feeling up to it."

He was a seasoned and gifted lay reader. Caught by the element of surprise, he looked at the Gospel. It was about Simon (Peter) and others who were fishing all night and caught nothing. Jesus showed up that the morning on the beach and told them to let down their nets for a catch. Simon's response was, "We have toiled all night and have caught nothing, nevertheless, at your word, we will let down the net."

Mr. Isaac singled out the word *nevertheless* and gave a powerful message. He thoroughly analyzed the word. The message was appropriate for me. Like the fishermen, I had toiled, not only the night before, but for several weeks, and caught nothing. Just when I was about to give up, the message came: nevertheless, at your word, I would let down the net once more. Sometimes, we must dig deep in the soil and remove all the roots before we can successfully transplant the plant.

The congregation was never told that the message was an impromptu one.

Mr. Isaac was very gracious to me in my infancy and saved me from embarrassment that Sunday. Twenty-five years later, I celebrated the Silver Jubilee of my ordination to the priesthood, at St. David's Church in Cambria Heights, New York. Mr. Isaac and a delegation of about twenty-five people from St. George's, Antigua, were present. He told the congregation about the "Nevertheless" sermon. Subsequently, he earned the name Nevertheless. At his funeral service, I had the honor of eulogizing him. The theme, of course, was "Nevertheless." One of the many things I learned from this story is humility: the ability to step aside and recognize the gifts of others in team ministry.

Humility is an important virtue, not to be confused with self-indulgent and personal deprivation, which is dehumanizing. I was determined not to be the victim of low self-esteem but, at the same time, not to be too haughty or proud. I endeavored to maintain a healthy, delicate balance. If the pendulum swings to either extreme, one seems foolish.

To counter the notion of insecurity and rejection, I took one of my recent ordination photographs and inscribed the following text below it. "I am fearfully and wonderfully made" (Psalm 139:14). The picture was placed on my dressing table. I looked at it morning and evening, and repeated the text. I used this to boost my self-esteem. Other affirmative statements I used were "I am a person of immense value. I can do all things through Christ, who strengthens me." It was very important in that era. The beginning of the end of colonialism, the decline of expatriate priests, and the advent of indigenous ones who were met with mixed feelings. Some were still holding on to the image of the white priests robed in white cassocks as they walked the streets, while others were heralding the dawn of West Indian clergy with the new shirt jack attire. Living on a small island where everyone seems to know each other, it was imperative that this new group of clergy bonded themselves for their survival. With God's providential guidance, not only did I learn to tread water, but I began swimming, or blooming where I was planted. The early hurdles were part of the growing process. It is like a newly transplanted plant, weathering the shock, with wilted leaves as it acclimatizes to its new environment. Once that is done, it begins to bloom.

In due time, God sent me a helper in the person of Enid, my wife. 1976 was an adventurous year, as indeed every year has been. As previously mentioned, the year began with my marriage to the parish (appointment as parish priest) on January 1, and on December 4 of the same year, Enid and I exchanged marital vows. Two marriages in one year. Overwhelming, isn't it? Our nuptials took place in Jamaica at the beginning of the Advent season, a season of hope. Our first Sunday in the parish after our marriage was December 18, the fourth Sunday in Advent. If you are familiar with the church's lectionary, you would know that the Gospel appointed for that day is about Mary and Joseph's engagement and Mary's pregnancy with the baby Jesus. What a day to introduce your wife to the congregation. When Enid and I were planning our marriage, we did not consult the lectionary. As noted earlier, "All things work together for good for those who love the Lord." In hindsight, just as Mary was pregnant with hope, so, too, Enid and I were pregnant with hope for the parish.

The Rev. J. Mastine Nisbett and Enid F. Gabbidon wedding ceremony Dec. 4th 1976

Before you get ahead of yourself, let me state unequivocally that Enid was not pregnant. We both were pregnant with hope for the parish. In a sense, you can say it was not Mary alone who was pregnant; Joseph and Mary were spiritually pregnant. They both cooperated with God's plan of salvation, as it should be. We all should be pregnant with God's spirit, pregnant with hope. Enid became my companion on this sacred journey. Like the Holy Family, Joseph, Mary, and the baby Jesus, who sought refuge in Egypt, St. George's was our refuge. Neither of us was from that country, but we adopted it as our home. While stationed in Antigua, I taught at the All Saints Secondary High School, fulfilling an earlier dream. We bloomed where we were planted, and God blessed us with three sons: Jason, Jevon, and Jereme.

Not only did our nuclear family bloom, but the parish family as well, insomuch that the bishop on two different occasions offered to transfer me to St. Anthony's Parish, Monserrat. This was considered a promotion, but I declined because our second son, Jevon, had an acute allergy and was still under the doctor's care. We wanted to stay in Antigua, where the medical facilities were supposedly better and air travel more accessible. We sojourned in Antigua for ten productive years, despite being thrown into the deep end of the pool. The marriage between the parish and me was mostly good and healthy. We established a long-lasting bond of fellowship. The congregants prided themselves in saying that they helped in my pastoral development.

One lesson I learned from the parish was an appreciation of the lay ministry. As a novice priest, I did not know everything, nor did I pretend to know it all. I recognized the gifts around me and utilized them where necessary. It was a mutual ministry. We all bloomed where we were planted. This is so vital. It is not the priest alone who should bloom where planted. The priest's role is to enable others to become who they are; that is, children of God. That means, among other things, blooming where God has planted them.

On reflection, I wondered whether Bishop Lindsay fully understood the wisdom of his decision to appoint me to be priest in charge of a parish immediately after graduating from seminary. Perhaps his decision was divinely inspired, as it should be. I do not think Bishop Lindsay knew that ten years later, I would be thrown into a comparable situation at St. David's in Cambria Heights, New York. What God was doing through the bishop was preparing me for the task ahead. Discernment, as was previously noted, is more like apprehending, not necessarily comprehending. We do not fully comprehend things at the time. Discernment is a process. It is not static; it is ongoing. One may be called to exercise a ministry at a specific place and at a precise time. At the completion of that specific ministry, one can be called to a new ministry elsewhere.

Shortly after I graduated from seminary in 1975, I wrote an article that was published in the *Angelus*, the Diocese of Antigua newspaper. In the article, I vowed to serve the people of the Caribbean. As stated earlier, it was the end of the colonial era and the rise of indigenous clergy. Ten years later, I answered the call to serve in the parish of St. David's in New York.

We already observed how a comparison could be made between the prophet Amos and myself. Now let us look at David the shepherd boy, the youngest son of Jesse, who was anointed to be the new king of Israel. The story is a familiar one: Samuel, the servant of the Lord, is sent to Jesse's house to choose one of Jesse's sons to be the new king. Jesse's first seven sons were not accepted. Samuel then asked Jesse if he had any more sons; he replied there was the youngest one, David, the shepherd boy who was out in the field, looking after the sheep. David was summoned to the house, and he, above everyone else, was chosen and anointed as the new king (1 Samuel:16). Now, that is absurd and ridiculous, you may say. In retrospect, my calling to the parish of St. David's was not different from David in the Old Testament.

One of the many priests who participated in my ordination to the priesthood was the late Rev. Henson Jacobs. He and the other priests and the bishop laid their hands on me, as is the custom in our church. Fr. Jacobs, who I met for the first time that day, was the rector of St. Augustine's Episcopal Church, in Brooklyn. He had a house in Antigua and visited the island frequently. St. George's was his adopted parish when he vacationed on the island.

I was under surveillance but had no idea that I was being observed. Fr. Jacobs obviously saw some spiritual growth in me and thought I would be a good candidate for St. David's Cambria Heights. He was the one who told me of the vacancy.

Migration to the United States was not on my radar. My first reaction to Fr. Jacobs's information was my initiation psalm from seminary, Psalm 131, the Psalm of Humility.

I spent much time in prayer, discernment, and meditating on Phillips Brooks's words:

> Do not pray for tasks equal to your powers.
> Pray for powers equal to the tasks.
> Then doing your work shall be no miracle.
> But you shall be a miracle.
> Every day you shall wonder at yourself,
> at the riches of life,
> which has come to you by the grace of God.
> (*Going up to Jerusalem*. Twenty Sermons, 1886, p. 330)

I submitted my application to St. David's. Fr. Jacobs was like the prophet Samuel, who went to Jesse's house in pursuit of a new leader to succeed King Saul. Jesse's older sons were like the candidates from the mainland who applied for the position. Yours truly was like the little boy David, Jesse's youngest son, who was occupied in the field. Note the distance between Antigua and Cambria Heights is almost eighteen hundred miles. That is way out in the field. Observe also that Fr. Jacobs not only introduced me to St. David's, but he also laid his hands on me at my ordination. In that sense, like Samuel, he anointed me then. I wonder whether when he saw me for the first time and laid his hands on me at the ordination, did he have any idea that he would refer me to St. David's Parish ten years later?

In May of 1984, I was invited by St. David's Search Committee to preach at a Sunday Eucharist and to be interviewed. I was one of the finalists and was cautiously optimistic. Recall the story of the prophet Amos, the dresser of sycamore trees, being called from the grafting of fruit trees to the grafting of souls. I thought there was some consistency in God's plan and wondered what was God up to now. Was God calling me to leave the countryside of Antigua to a ministry in the Big Apple? Is not that absurd? But then, have not all my interactions with God thus far, on the surface, seem to be ridiculous and foolish? I decided to accept the invitation to visit St. David's, even though I had some financial constraints; Enid and I were expecting our third child. In faith, I made a radical investment, using our meager resources to travel to the America.

Fr. Jacobs was very generous with his hospitality and hosted me on my brief visit. Above everything else, though, Fr. Jacobs was an excellent coach. He must have seen my nervousness and anxiety. I was a bundle of nerves.

"Just be yourself," he said, "and imagine yourself at St. George's Antigua near the seaside."

Both the sermon and the interview went well, I thought. After my brief visit, I returned to Antigua.

"How did it go?" Enid asked.

"I don't know," I replied.

"What do you mean, you don't know?"

"I did the best I can, and now it's in the Lord's hands."

The next six months were emotionally challenging. There was joy in the expectancy of our third child. There was anxiety of being called as the new rector of St. David's. Added to these emotions, there was sadness and grief with the decline of my father's health. He was hospitalized shortly after Jereme was born, and I traveled frequently to Nevis to visit him. The sound of the telephone ignited certain emotions within me: particularly when they were overseas calls. Was it a call from St. David's Church, New York, informing me whether I was elected or rejected? There were two possible emotions. Was the telephone call from Nevis, informing me about my father's demise? Still another type of emotion. Then, of course, there was the joy of the birth of our third son, coupled with the sibling rivalry of our two older boys. Note, I have not mentioned anything about my parochial duties or my part-time teaching in all this emotional roller coaster.

If Fr. Jacobs was the Samuel, then the late Stanley Gordon was like the angel Gabriel, who was the bearer of good news to Mary, the mother of our Lord. In December 1984, I received a telephone call from Stanley, the chairman of the Search Committee, informing me that I was elected to be the new rector of St. David's. Not only was it the month of December, but it was in the middle of the Advent season; the lectionary text for that week was Luke's account of the angel Gabriel visiting Mary and saluting her: "Hail! You are highly favored. The Lord is with you.... you will conceive in your womb and bear a son, and you will call his name Jesus" (Luke 1:28–31).

Like Mary, I was startled and confused. In a submissive faith, I quietly responded, "Be it unto me according to your word" (Luke 1:38).

In putting all these pieces together, I can now understand Jevon's illness while we sojourned in Antigua, and my turning down two offers to be transferred to St. Anthony, Monserrat. Had I gone to Monserrat, I would have probably lost contact with Samuel, Fr. Jacobs.

A week later, on Sunday, December 23, 1984, the fourth Sunday of Advent, the telephone rang again. This time, it was my father's passing. He was hospitalized a few days after my son's birth and died a week after my election as rector. So many different emotions, culminating with the joy of Christmas.

My father's death was a critical point in my life. His passing reminds me of Moses's death. At Mt. Nebo, Moses sees the Promised Land but knows that he will not live to enter it; he passed on his mantle to Joshua, his successor. Clarence, my father, was like Moses, passing on the mantle to me, Joshua; ironically, Clarence's father was also named Joshua. He (Clarence) stood between the two Joshuas: father and son. My father was like Moses, who earlier received the mantle from Joshua and then passed on the mantle to me. Six weeks after the burial of my father (Moses), I began my journey to the United States, the Promised Land, where I was to discover and live out the true meaning of my name, Joshua.

My grief over my father's death was coupled with severing my relationship with St. George's parish, creating a double sorrow. But the grief was mixed with joy at the birth of our third son, Jereme, and the expectancy of the new parish in New York. Holding these two emotions of joy and sadness was typical of a priest. Yes, I do recall officiating at a wedding ceremony and a funeral service the same day; I rejoiced with a family at the birth of a child and then anointed someone at the end of their life.

Wrestling with these emotions has not always been easy. In one sense, I want to be present and empathize with someone, but at the same time, I am only human, and I cannot carry everyone's burden; only Christ can do that. I am not the Savior of the world; that position is filled, and there is no vacancy. My role in such a situation is to hold a healthy balance between being engaged and disengaged with the person. If you do not, you can easily get burnt out.

I was now dealing with these emotions in my personal life. I was the object, the one subjected to the pain, and it hurt. I now understood the counselee's dilemma. Hopefully, it will make me a better counselor. God is always working out his divine purpose, weaving our joys and pains to create a beautiful tapestry in the universe. You and I are just privileged to be part of it. St. Luke records Mary's revolutionary song she sang while visiting her cousin Elizabeth: "My soul magnifies the Lord," but alas, her joy was short-lived. In the second chapter of Luke, the evangelist reported that there was no room in the inn in Bethlehem for Mary and Joseph. Consequently, they had to resort to a stable. That is where the Christ Child was born.

In a somewhat comparable situation, just as my family and I began to prepare for the journey to New York, I received a very disturbing telephone call. I had been named rector of the parish and signed a contractual agreement, but I was then instructed not to travel with my family to the United States. There was no room in the inn. I should leave them behind and arrange for them to join me later. I was shocked, disillusioned, and annoyed. The joy of the call turned into sadness. I wondered whether they had second thoughts. Did they want to get out of the contract, by instructing me not to bring my family? Was it to discourage me, in the hope that I would withdraw from the contract? All these questions invaded my mind. My world was turned upside down. I had already resigned from my positions in the diocese, my part-time teaching, and secretary of the Antigua Christian Council. I had said good-bye to the television audience on my monthly show, *Common Ground*.

The parish was already planning a farewell party, and our flights had been booked. What were we supposed to do now? This was embarrassing. It would certainly make us look foolish. What did they expect me to do, leave my family behind? Neither of us were from Antigua. These people were playing with our emotions. I was terrified.

At Enid's suggestion, we called her brother George, who lived in the Bronx, New York, and told him our dilemma. He readily agreed to temporarily host Enid and the children while they sorted things out at the church. Enid's sisters, Pearla and Janet, also lived in the Bronx and concurred with the plans. I recalled the story of the wise men who were warned in a dream not to return to Herod because of his devious plans to destroy the baby Jesus. Consequently, they returned home by another route. Likewise, guided by the Holy Spirit, we proceeded as previously planned.

How could I leave my family in Antigua? Joseph did not leave Mary and the baby Jesus in Egypt. No, he took them with him. I likewise vowed to take my family with me. That started another chapter in our lives: "Living on the Edge." It was like walking on a tightrope across Niagara Falls. It was risky. It was adventurous. It was like walking on water with our Lord. It was durable, with God's divine protection. It demanded a radical trust in the Lord.

The Rev J. Mastine and Mrs. Nisbett with their sons Jason, Jevon, and Jereme.

CHAPTER 4

LIVING ON THE EDGE

In the previous chapter we observed that David, the youngest son of Jesse, was anointed to replace Saul as king of Israel. However, the latter half of 1 Samuel tells us this was not a done deal. During those troublesome years, Saul pursued David, even to the point of wanting to kill him. David was more popular than Saul. Note the song of the women: "Saul has killed his thousands, and David his ten thousand" (1 Samuel 18:7).

Life for David was like living on the edge.

Jesus spent forty days in the wilderness, fasting and praying. Three times, he was confronted by the devil to choose between good and evil. He chose good. This is nothing short of living on the edge. Additionally, Luke referred to the first sermon Jesus preached in his hometown synagogue, in Nazareth. There was much rejection that day. He was thrown out of the synagogue, "and they led him to the brow of the hill on which their town was built, so that they might hurl him off the cliff. But he passed through the midst of them and went on his way" (Luke 4:29–30).

Jesus spent his life living on the edge. His opponents were constantly looking for occasions to entrap him in his conversation to get rid of him. Even on the cross and at his death, he stood on the edge of life. Ultimately, he crossed over into a new life, as the Resurrected Christ.

My initial encounter with St. David's was nothing less than living on the edge. When I arrived in New York on February 6, 1985, my body immediately went into a shock. The temperature was about 10 degrees, and there was a foot of snow on the ground. Coming from a tropical island where the average temperature is about 85 degrees, it felt like walking from a sauna into a cold storage room. It was my first winter experience. Jason and Jevon were excited by the snow. Jereme, still a baby, wrapped in swaddling clothes, screamed when his aunt removed the blanket to see his face. Enid, on the other hand, had already experienced winter, having lived in England. The shock was not only physical, it was emotional as well. Five hours earlier, I had said goodbye to the parishioners in Antigua. Now I was saying hello to another parish family. But the one that hurt most was saying goodbye to my nuclear family, although they were going to be only twenty miles away in the Bronx, while I stayed at the rectory. Sleep did not attend me during my first few nights. Restlessness was the order of the night. The only things that visited me were these haunting questions: What are you doing here? Where is your family? Are you sure you made the right decision?

I had a small transistor radio in my bedroom, which kept my ceremony at night. Strangely, during my third night at the rectory, I was awakened from a catnap by Brook Benton singing.

> Fools rush in where angels fear to tread....
> Fools rush in where wise men
> never, never, never go....
> Open up your heart and let this fool rush in.

Oh, my God. That was who I was: a fool.

Two days later, the Old Testament lesson appointed for the morning prayer was 1 Kings 19. Here, Elijah found himself discouraged and lying under a juniper tree, begging God to take his life. His life was not taken. Instead, God renewed his hope and faith. This passage resonated well with me.

I felt imprisoned and in exile, separated from my family in a new country. Reflecting on it now, it was like our Lord having been baptized, anointed with the Holy Spirit, and declared God's beloved Son, only to

Bloom Wherever God Plants You

be sent into the wilderness to be tested by Satan. And believe me, there were many, many tests. Being separated from my family at the onset of our sojourn in New York reminded me of the atrocities of the African heritage. The Europeans, in a deliberate effort to destroy the African family structure, separated family members on their arrival in the New World. *Oh, my God. Is this for real?* I thought. *Am I reliving history?*

But the separation also reminded me of the Holy Family's flight into Egypt to escape the wrath of King Herod (Matthew 2:13–22). In like manner, my family took refuge in the Bronx until an opportune time to join me in Cambria Heights. This was quite troubling, to say the least, but it was only a sign of things to come.

The annals record the first service of St. David's Parish was held on February 11, 1940 (Founder's Day). Ironically, my first Sunday in the parish as the new rector was February 10, 1985, exactly forty-five years after its founding. The number 45 is interesting because the land on which our church building is presently located was bought in 1945, and exactly forty years later, I was called as the second rector. We are sure having fun with these numbers and dates, aren't we?

That being said, my first Sunday in the parish was quite a test. I was informed before the service that I did not have to preach. Just bring a word of greeting, I was told.

I was surprised but did not question it, even though I thought it was strange. Why wouldn't the congregation expect a sermon from their new rector? I said nothing, assuming the supply priest, who was present, would preach. However, my intuitive feeling told me to bring a copy of my sermon with me. That I did.

Much to my surprise, during the hymn before the Gospel, I was told, "We are expecting you to deliver the sermon today."

"You have to be crazy," I replied. "You told me earlier that I did not have to preach."

"It is your call, brother."

I was overwhelmed with shock and grew more and more nervous.

"Lord," I prayed, *"if ever I need your help, it is now. Assist me to proclaim your Gospel."*

With much fear and trembling, I approached the pulpit. I took a quick glance at my family, who worshiped with us that morning, and began to proclaim the message. From that point, the Holy Spirit took over. It was like becoming unconscious and unaware of the immediate surroundings. Yes, I had a manuscript and had spent several weeks preparing the address, but in the final analysis, I was merely the vessel, as I should be, and God was the potter. Shocked as I was, but no time to deal with emotions, I proceeded with my address.

I recalled another occasion, when I was called to Clair Foster's home to pray for her daughter, Michelle, who was critically ill. I laid my hands on the young lady, and her mother, who has since passed on, placed her hands on mine, as I prayed. The prayer lasted for a while. I felt empty and exhausted when I left the house. I said nothing to Enid, who was waiting for me. The following Sunday, Clair testified in church about the miracle that she experienced in her home. She spoke about my prayer, the changing of my voice and countenance, but more so the healing of Michelle.

The text I preached on that day came from Luke 4:8–19: "The spirit of the Lord is upon me, because he has anointed me to bring good news to the poor. He has sent me to release the captives and recovery of sight to the blind, to let the oppressed go free, to proclaim the year of our Lord." This was not part of the lectionary reading for the day, but I specifically chose it for my first Sunday as the new rector. The text, of course, was part our Lord's inaugural address, referred to earlier. Strangely enough, Jesus was rejected in his hometown when he preached on that text. Now, I too, encountered my own rejection. That morning, the confusion over my preaching or not preaching gave me a feeling of rejection. I was reminded of St. John in his prologue, speaking about Jesus saying, "He came unto his own and his own received him not" (John 1:11).

Before the day was over, I felt another sense of rejection. Cy Jordan thought it was a good idea that I attend the funeral service for Reverend Farley. He was the Archdeacon of Queens and rector of St. Luke's Forest Hills. We arrived early that Sunday afternoon, stood inside the church building, and waited to be seated; meanwhile, the ushers busily escorted others to their seats. I do not know whether the seats were limited and reserved. But no one said anything to us. True, I was not well known in the diocese, hardly there for a week, but I was dressed in a recognizable clergy shirt, though that should not make a difference. As children of God, we are equal human beings in the Lord's house. The text that resonated with me that afternoon was, "I was a stranger and you did not take me in" (Matthew 26:43). Cy was very apologetic. I tried to reassure him that I was fine, and it was no fault of his. Deep down within me, I was saying to myself, *if you only knew what I previously encountered that day*. Like Mary, I pondered them over in my heart (Luke 2:19) and shared my story only with my wife, as I continued living on the edge.

Meetings in the vestry were tense, and I did not look forward to them. Living in the rectory was like living in the wilderness, isolated from my family. Then there was the ghost of my predecessor, the late Reverend Leo Malania; many parishioners revered him and spoke fondly of him often; perhaps they were not yet ready for a new rector.

In addition to all that, there was the problem of prejudice. That, too, I experienced when a parishioner, speaking about the supply priest, referred to him as a "white man." Now, the priest was certainly black but of a lighter complexion than I was. What she said to me that day suggested that his color made a difference to her, since I was black. The prejudice was due to ignorance. Much like what I experienced in the Diocese of Fredericton, New Brunswick, Canada. Visiting several parishes in that diocese, I observed photographs from various parishes in my home diocese, displayed in our companion diocese. Sadly, the pictures were showing the poorest of the poor. Being an ambassador for my diocese, I found it difficult and humiliating. Folks asked me, "Do you live in trees? When did you learn to speak English? Since you came to Canada?"

What confirmed the ignorance was a foot-washing ceremony as part of the liturgy. The campers were white. I was the only black person in attendance. Everyone was asked to wash the feet of the person seated next to them. I could see the young lady nervously holding my foot and probably wishing she could play the game of musical chairs and escape the embarrassment of washing my feet. The other campers looked on eagerly. Their looks were so intense, I think they were looking to see whether the washing of my feet would make them less black. Their mouths opened wide, apparently surprised that the color of my feet did not change. It was a teachable moment. I remembered Sidney Poitier in that classical film *To Sir, with Love*. Sidney played the role of Mark Thackeray, a black teacher in a London East End school. The teacher hurt himself and began bleeding. The students, who were white, rushed to see the color of the blood and were surprised to learn that his blood was red like theirs. The late Dr. Martin Luther King Jr. was right when he said, "Nothing in all the world is more dangerous than sincere ignorance and conscientious stupidity" (Brainy Quotes).

The individual who appeared to have been prejudiced was kind and generous toward my family, once the supply priest was off the scene. It became apparent to me that there were factions within the parish. It seems that once I was elected and called to the parish, there was a group who preferred the supply priest, while others supported me. Life for me was like Daniel, who was thrown into the den of lions to test his allegiance to God. The Lord honored Daniel's loyalty by sending three friends: Shadrach, Meshach, and Abednego. Likewise, God sent me some cheerleaders, including George, my brother-in-law, Pearla and Janet, my sisters-in-law, and a host of parishioners who supported and encouraged me during those challenging times.

Many of them transported me to and from the Bronx to see my family. Visiting my family, at times, felt like seeing someone in the hospital or an institution with visiting hours. At the end of the visit, you reluctantly must say goodbye to your loved one. In reflection, I thank God for giving me faith like Daniel. Someone said, "People are like teabags; you never know how strong you are until you are placed in hot water."

The greatest test came one day while I was meditating on the Old Testament lesson for the upcoming Sunday. It was about Abraham being summoned by God to take his son, Isaac, to Mt. Moriah and offer him there as a sacrifice to the Lord. It is amazing how the lectionary readings, which are prearranged, oftentimes mirrored my personal experiences. They were like my spiritual compasses. First, the angel Gabriel visits Mary and Joseph to inform them of their role in the coming of the Messiah. The lesson coincided with Enid and me at our first Sunday in St. George's Antigua as a newlywed couple. The second, somewhat like the first, is the angel Gabriel saluting Mary, "Hail, you are highly favored. You have been chosen to be the Mother of our Lord." The text resonated with Stanley Gordon, chair of St. David's Search Committee, calling to inform me that I had been highly favored and was elected rector of the parish.

This one, though, blew my mind. I was bewildered, numb, and angry. While meditating on the sacrifice of Isaac, the telephone rang. Enid was on the line. I could hear crying in the background. Her voice was cracking.

"Mastine, you must come now. We have to rush Jevon to the hospital."

"What happened?" I asked.

"I cannot talk now. His stomach is distended, and he is in a lot of pain."

"Okay, I will try to get there as fast as I can."

The doorbell rang. It was a Sylvester Fauconier, an angel, who came at the right time and readily agreed to transport me to the Bronx.

"Father," he said as we drove off, "you seem to be having a rough time."

"This is not a rough time," I replied. "This is hell."

"What do you do in hell?"

"Get out alive as fast as you can."

He recognized I was not in the mood for conversation, and he quietly respected my wish. I was haunted by the Mt. Moriah story.

Oh, my God, what are you doing to me? Are you asking me to be like Abraham? Is St. David's my Moriah? Is Jevon the Isaac you are asking me to sacrifice? Oh, God, please do not do that to us.

I prayed and prayed. I was perspiring in the dead of winter.

"Are you okay?" Sylvester asked.

"Yes, just get me to the hospital as fast as you can. Oh, my God, what have I done?*Was I foolish to bring my family here, to be subjected to this nightmare? Maybe I should have left them behind to join me later. Or maybe I should have called off the contract and remained in Antigua. It might have been better to stay and recover from the humiliation rather than coming here and losing my son."*

I began fantasizing being back in Antigua. I remember my farewell service. It was Sunday, February 2, 1985, and the Feast of the Presentation of our Lord in the temple. The Most Reverend Orland Lindsay, who ordained me as deacon and priest, was the celebrant and preacher. Suddenly, I recalled the Gospel for that day. The aged prophet Simeon, blessing the baby Jesus and prophesying to Mary, said, "This child is destined for the falling and the rising of many, in Israel, and to be the sign that will be opposed. So that the inner thoughts of many will be revealed—and a sword will pierce your own soul too" (Luke 2:34–35). This was part of the

Gospel I read that morning. Bishop Lindsay, like the old prophet Simeon, blessed my family and me as we prepared to make our departure. Now, a few weeks later, the "sword has pierced through my soul." I recalled the last hymn we sung that morning:

> Lead me, guide me along the way.
> For if you lead me, I cannot stray.
> Lord, let me walk each day with thee.
> Lead me, oh Lord, lead me.

I paused. Then I suddenly said, "Oh, my God, are you really leading me to Mt. Moriah?"

There was traffic congestion on the Throgs Neck Bridge, and I grew more anxious. Suddenly, I recalled when Jevon had his first allergy attack, in Antigua. We rushed him to the hospital. The doctor decided to admit him overnight for observation. Enid, being a nurse, asked the doctor if she should give him some Benadryl. The doctor concurred, and the child's swelling immediately subsided.

"Lord, send us another miracle," I prayed.

The traffic was at a standstill. There was an accident on the road. I was frustrated, angry, and anxious. Something must have told Sylvester to turn the car radio' to the family radio station. It was the right thing to do, for this hymn was aired at that time:

> Guide me, O thou Great Jehovah,
> pilgrim through this barren land.
> I am weak but thou art mighty.
> Hold me with thy powerful hand.
> Bread of heaven, bread of heaven,
> feed me now and evermore.

In Antigua, almost everyone knew each other. The hospital was a regular work site. I could probably close my eyes and walk through it. Not so at North Central Hospital, which was my first hospital to visit in this country. After being lost and confused, I eventually found Enid and Jevon in the emergency room. The child's stomach was completely distended, like a pregnant woman about to deliver a baby. The only thing was, the rest of his body was that of a five-year-old child, looking sad and worried. We all held hands, and I prayed. I anointed Jevon and tried to assure him that he was going to get better.

A young doctor entered the room. After reviewing his records and examining him, she said,

"The child is poisoned."

"Poisoned?" I asked. "What do you mean by that?"

"He is overmedicated."

I was livid. "How did that happen?"

"Well, your physician prescribed 2.5 mg suppositories, but the pharmacist, in error, gave him 25 mg."

"What? You have to be crazy."

"Not me. You mean your pharmacist."

"What? What kind of crack pharmacist is this? This would not even happen in Antigua."

"We must flush out his stomach and get that medication out of him. It may take a couple of days."

The next few days were stressful for my family, but awfully painful for Jevon, who was constantly vomiting what looked like thick dark chocolate. When he was not vomiting, he was having diarrhea or doing both at the same time. This reminded me of my experience as a teenager, when I almost drowned. After being unconscious for a while, I found myself on the beach, vomiting.

Jevon was hooked up to all kinds of machines, as they tried to flush his stomach and keep him hydrated. Watching him lying helplessly on that bed, I could not stop thinking of Abraham and Isaac at Mt. Moriah.

"Oh, God, please provide a lamb for the sacrifice, and save our son," I prayed.

It was now evening, and Jevon was resting. Enid and I were alone. We looked at each other. Her eyes were red, her hair disheveled, and there was an anguished look on her face. The past four weeks had been exceedingly trying for her, coping with our three young children, while I adjusted myself at the rectory. Were it not for her brother and sisters, I do not know how we would have managed.

"Mastine," Enid said, "I don't know about you, but I have serious doubts whether we made the right decision to come to America."

"Why do you say that?"

"Look at all we have been through. We have been treated like refugees. Look at that nasty stunt they pulled on you on the first Sunday. And now, look at Jevon, lying helpless on that hospital bed. Are you blind? This is hell."

I realized that she was completely overwhelmed. She needed to vent her feelings. I, too, had my doubts, but I suppose because of my male ego, or better still, my faith, I managed to tread water in the deep ocean of life. I needed to support her and provide some buoyancy for her spirit. Giving in to her fears would do no good.

"Yes, we have been tried," I said, "and yes, we have experienced hell on earth. But although we might have been treated as refugees, your brother and sisters took us in. We are not homeless. When there was no room in the inn, Uncle George provided his stable. As for the stunt they pulled on me, the Lord provided a way of escape. With regards to Jevon, do you remember when he was a baby and had his first allergy attack? We rushed him to the hospital. When the doctor said she would admit him for observation, do you remember what you told her?"

She paused and sobbed, "Yes, I asked her if she would consider giving him some Benadryl."

"Absolutely, and that was what saved his life. So, nurse, you better come up with another prescription."

Drying her tears, she smiled, and we embraced each other, tearfully but with a ray of hope. She said, "You always make it sound so simple."

"I am not trivializing this hellish experience, but I'm not going to let it overcome me."

As we continue to embrace each other, we prayed. In my prayer, I said,

"Oh, God, here we are in the emergency room of this hospital, because we have an emergency. Oh, God, we need you, and we need you urgently. Oh, God, make speed to save us. Oh, Lord,

make haste to help us. Amen."

Enid left for home shortly thereafter to relieve her sisters, who were babysitting for us. I spent the night at the hospital but did not get much sleep. I just kept vigil, answering Jevon's questions:

"When am I going home?"
"I do not know, son, but we hope soon."

Jevon

That short dialogue was an ah-ha moment, a lightbulb. It resonated with Isaac's question: "My father, behold the wood and the fire; where is the lamb?"

Abraham replied, "God will provide a lamb."

It became the springboard for my upcoming sermon. Amazing how God speaks to us, even in crises.

The following day, the supply priest offered to preach at the Sunday's liturgy, fearing that I was overwhelmed. I thanked him for his thoughtfulness but assured him that it would not be necessary, for I already had the sermon. Two days later, on Sunday, I preached on the Old Testament lesson appointed for the day, Genesis 22:1–14: Abraham being asked by God to offer his son, Isaac, as a sacrifice. This was the most challenging sermon I had ever preached. The sacrifice of your son on God's altar. This was not just another biblical story, read in the abstract, as something that occurred in ancient history. On the contrary, this was real. I literally relived the story. St. David's was my Mt. Moriah, and the hospital bed was the altar where my son lay, ready to be sacrificed.

"Daddy, when am I going home?"

"Soon, I hope, son."

"What is taking it so long?"

"We want you to get well."

"How long will that be?"

Isaac said to his father, Abraham, "Behold, the fire and the word; but where is the lamb for the burnt offering?"

Abraham replied, "God will provide a lamb for the burnt offering."

As I wrestled with that text, I felt reassured that God would intervene and save Jevon's life, as he did with Isaac. That reassurance was based on the Lord's steadfast love for humankind, as demonstrated in the epistle for that day:

> What then are we to say about these things? If God is for us, who is against us? He who did not withhold his own Son, but gave him up for all of us, will he not with him also give us everything else? Who will bring any charge against God's elect? It is God who justifies. Who is to condemn? It is Christ Jesus, who died, yes, who was raised, who is at the right hand of God, who indeed intercedes for us. Who will separate us from the love of Christ? Will hardship, or distress, or persecution, or famine, or nakedness, or peril, or sword? As it is written, "For your sake we are being killed all day long; we are accounted as sheep to be slaughtered." No, in all these things we are more than conquerors through him who loved us. For I am convinced that neither death, nor life, nor angels, nor rulers, nor things present, nor things to come, nor powers, nor height, nor depth, nor anything else in all creation, will be able to separate us from the love of God in Christ Jesus our Lord. (Romans 8:31–39)

Yes, absolutely nothing can separate us from the love of God. At the end of the service, the supply priest said to me, "You are one hell of a man."

"What do you mean by that?" I asked.

"For you to preach on that text, in your present situation, you have to be strong."

I replied, "It is not about you or me; it is about God."

Over the next few days, I continued to ponder the text. What kind of God can demand that people sacrifice their son? Is not that barbaric? How does that measure up with human rights today? Was Abraham a fool to believe that God was asking him to sacrifice his son? Was he schizophrenic? Was he mentally deranged? But the worst of all, was this a fellowship of fools that I was initiated into? Fools for Christ? Reflecting on the word *fool*, I recalled Paul's letter to the Corinthians: "The foolishness of God is wiser than man's wisdom" (1 Corinthians 1:25–31).

"Okay, God, if your wisdom is truly wiser than man's wisdom, why don't you show me?"

A sense of guilt reigned over me for a while. Was I putting God to the test? That evening, I had an epiphany. It was like a voice saying to me, "The child lying in the hospital bed was my child before he became your child." *Amazing*, I thought. *What a powerful revelation.* The next day, Jevon was discharged from the hospital.

Well, if that was not amazing, how would you describe this? This manuscript came to a sudden halt with that last sentence: "The next day, Jevon was discharged from the hospital." It was the last sentence I wrote on Delta Airlines en route to JFK from Barcelona, Spain, on May 7, 2018. Twelve hours after Enid and I returned from our vacation, we received a telephone call informing us that our youngest son, Jereme, was hospitalized. No time for jet lag and unpacking of luggage. We must be up and going. He had been hospitalized with acute pancreatitis. So critical was his illness that he spent four days in ICU in excruciating pain. It was like déjà vu all over again. Keeping the vigil at the hospital bedside, a replay of our family crisis thirty-three years ago.

The ICU at Northwell Long Island Jewish Hospital was a familiar place for me. I have visited many patients and administered the last rites to many individuals on this unit. Now I was here for my son, and I could not stop thinking of the many people I anointed there.

Jereme was in a private room. Directly across from him was an older gentleman.

A nurse entered the room and said,

"Sorry, we are going to keep the curtain drawn for a while."

She closed the curtain and left the room. The curtain remained closed for about an hour.

"The guy over there passed," Jereme said.

I held his hand and said, "Yes, he did."

There were at least three patients who died on that unit during Jereme's brief stay. We were all happy when he was discharged. It was like the Valley of the Shadow of Death. Living on the edge, but it is that very edge where you are called to bloom.

On May 19, 2018, millions watched the royal wedding of Prince Harry and Meghan Markle. Many were in awe with the dynamic sermon, "Discover the Power of Love and Fire," by the Most Reverend Michael Bruce Curry, presiding bishop of the Episcopal Church. The next day was Pentecost Day, and I adapted the theme from Bishop Curry and preached on the topic, "Discover the Power of the Wind" (the Holy Spirit). It was all related to the sound of the rushing mighty wind at Pentecost (Acts 2).

That evening, I visited Jereme in the hospital. He was resting when I arrived. On his awakening, he reached out his hand to me and asked, in a very low voice,

"Daddy, where is the wind?"

I asked, "What are you talking about?"

"The wind that you spoke about this morning." He had watched the service on YouTube. In the sermon, I made several references to the work of the Holy Spirit in Acts of the Apostles and within our local congregation, including the healing of Michelle Foster, referred to earlier in this chapter. Mention was made of a unique experience in the Holy Land at Mount Beatitude. I was presiding at a Eucharist for people who were on a pilgrimage with me. It was an early morning outdoor service, facing the Galilean Sea. We were constantly bombarded with gusts of wind during the homily. My vestments were being blown over my head, and the altar linens were being blown away.

Impulsively, I stretched out my right hand and said, "Peace, be still." Nothing happened. Everyone laughed. "What did you expect?" I asked. "Only Jesus can quiet the storm."

After I said that, the wind immediately ceased, and we continued the service peacefully. The pilgrims were all in awe, claiming they had witnessed a miracle that morning.

Jereme's question that evening, "Daddy, where is the wind?" was profound. It reminded me of Jevon's interrogating question thirty-three years ago: "Daddy, when am I going home?" And of course, it reminded me of Isaac's question to his father Abraham, "Behold the wood and the fire; where is the lamb?"

Jereme

I told Jereme, "I cannot catch the wind, but God's Spirit is always around us."

The Holy Spirit was present when Jevon was a baby in the hospital in Antigua. The Holy Spirit was also present with Jevon when he was hospitalized at North Central Hospital.

The Holy Spirit was most present with your daughter, Alana, who was born five years ago at a birthweight of one pound fourteen ounces. The Holy Spirit sustained her during the eight months she was hospitalized. Do you remember the baby with two IVs in her navel, one in her foot, a monitor on each side of her chest, and a respirator and feeding tube in her mouth? Now she is five years old. Your daughter is a fighter. She is a survivor. You can learn a lesson from her. I did not bring you the wind because the Holy Spirit is already here, but I brought you two candles.

Alana

Earlier that afternoon, in a memorial and thanksgiving service for the Friends of Trelawny Association, fourteen candles were lit for the former members who had died during the past year. While I complimented them for this memorial act of kindness, I challenged them to light their individual candles and become who they are: the light of the world.

"Take your lighted candle into the dark world and let it shine," I said.

There were enough candles for everyone. I took two of these candles for Jereme, to light up his bedside and give him a ray of hope. Four days later, like the Pentecostal wind, "the spirit blew him out of the hospital"; he was finally discharged after sixteen days. Excited over his release, he texted his friends, "Free at last, thank God Almighty, I am free at last." Was he really free? No. At least not yet. Four days later, he was readmitted to the hospital for a brief two-day stay as we, along with him, continued living on the edge.

At 7:30 a.m. on Sunday, June 10, 2018, as I was leaving home for the morning Eucharist, the telephone rang. It was Jereme, informing me that he had been readmitted to the hospital. This was his third admission in hospital in one month. The young man was exasperated by his debilitating illness, and so were we, the caregivers. How do you lead in worship under such a stressful situation? Had it not been for my priestly duties, I would have gone immediately to the hospital. I was stuck like the priest in the parable of the Good Samaritan (Luke 10), who hastened to the temple to execute his priestly duties, leaving a man half-dead on the Jericho Road, desperately in need of help. With no able assistant who can relieve me in that eleventh hour, I prayed with my son and assured him we would remember him at the Eucharist. As I hung up the phone and traveled to the church building, I prayed, "Oh, God, here am I, on my way to church to exalt your name, and my son is hospitalized for the third time. We have cried out to you, and yet he continues to suffer. As we offer the Holy Sacrifice to you this day, I pray that you may speedily help to relieve Jereme of his suffering, and we entrust him to your everlasting care."

On arrival at the church building, I told no one about Jereme's hospitalization, lest it become a distraction in worship. I conscientiously tried to focus on the worship, but it was difficult. The collect for purity reads,

"Almighty God, to you all hearts are open, all desires known, and from you, no secrets are hid: Cleanse the thoughts of our hearts by the inspiration of your Holy Spirit, that we may perfectly love you and worthily magnify your holy name."

The prayer was prayed most earnestly, but I must admit I kept thinking about my suffering son throughout the liturgy. By the grace of God, I was able to execute my duties. At the end of the service, I informed the congregation of Jereme's admission to the hospital. The second service was a replica of the first, except during the singing of the post-Communion hymn, "What a Friend We Have in Jesus," the singing was lusty. I felt the pulse of the congregation. It boosted my spiritual adrenaline. The stanza that really ministered to me was:

> Have we trials and temptations? Is there trouble anywhere?
> We should never be discouraged; take it to the Lord in prayer.
> Can we find a friend so faithful who will all our sorrows share?
> Jesus knows our every weakness; take it to the Lord in prayer.

For the next seven days, Jereme remained in the hospital, living on the edge. Finally, on the sixth day, his gallbladder was removed, and he was discharged the following day. The Gospel appointed for Sunday, July 1, 2018, was Mark 5:21–43. This passage was about the raising of Jairus's daughter. Jairus was a leader of the synagogue. He pleaded with our Lord to heal his daughter, who eventually died before the Lord arrived at his house. Miraculously, Jesus restored the little girl's life and ordered the family to give her something to eat.

Ironically, this was Jereme's first public worship with the congregation since his illness. Like Jairus, we prayed for God's divine intervention. The prayer group convened nightly. Individuals made intercessions to God on behalf of our son, who was standing on the precipice of life, living on the edge. Jesus told Jairus's family to give the resurrected girl something to eat. Coincidentally, Jereme ate very little during the six weeks of his illness. He began eating after returning home. The amazing thing in all of this was, we witnessed the dramatizing of the scripture in our presence. Living on the edge, and blooming where we are planted, even in adversity. It required a radical trust in God.

CHAPTER 5

DO NOT QUIT; GET FIT

It should not be perceived that the radical trust in God was spontaneous. Oh, yes, there were times I doubted, like doubting Thomas, especially in those early days, when I was extremely tested. My bedroom was my war room, where I argued with God. With all that my family had endured, I wanted to know exactly what God's plan was for us. Why were we tested like that? When would it be over? When was enough, enough? Should I quit or stay? We human beings tend to pray more earnestly when we desperately need something, when we have been diagnosed with cancer, are confronted with a natural disaster, or are about to attend a job interview, then we pray with much enthusiasm.

Like the psalmist, we pray from the depth of our being: "Out of the depths I cry to you, O Lord, Lord, hear my voice. Let your ears be attentive to the voice of my supplications" (Psalm 130:1–2).

Arguing or bargaining with God is nothing new. The Israelites did it when Abraham learned that God was about to destroy Sodom and Gomorrah, which was the hometown of his nephew, Lot. He bargained with God. He asked God if a certain number of people were found to be righteous, would he spare them? Abraham kept bargaining with God until the number decreased from fifty righteous people to ten. The back-and-forth arguing with the Lord saved Lot's family (Genesis 18:16–32).

When the prophet Isaiah visited King Hezekiah, who was critically ill, the king was told that he was about to die and should get his house in order. Hezekiah wept and pleaded with God for his life. The king's prayer did not go unnoticed by God; God heard the prayer and allowed him to live another fifteen years (2 Kings 20:1–11). In the New Testament, Mary, the mother of our Lord, interceded on behalf of the newly wedded couple, who were short on wine. Jesus responded in the affirmative and provided an abundance of wine (John 2:1–12).

What we can conclude from these stories is that God does care about our needs. Jesus said whatsoever we ask in His name, He will grant us (Matthew 7:7). Since the omniscient God knows beforehand the outcome of our decisions and petitions, maybe it is not so much that God had a change of mind, but that God knows what the final decision will be. We can argue with God to intercede on behalf of others because God is gracious and loves interacting with us. Case in point: Jacob wrestled with God (Genesis 32:22–32).

There is nothing wrong in praying for God to change our circumstances. However, we must remember, as blogger Zachary Perkins reminds us, that we are part of a larger story. God is "weaving a beautiful tapestry in the world and every blessing or tragedy is meant to bring every thread to work together in perfect harmony" (Relevant Magazine.com).

In my case, I am eternally grateful that our prayers for Jevon were answered. Our son's life was saved; but I still had the lingering doubts about whether I should I stay or quit.

Someone wrote,

"When care is pressing you down a bit, rest if you must, but don't quit. Success is failure turned inside out" (Truth Follower.com).

WHY I STAYED

Years ago, sharing my early experiences at St. David's with my classmates at Sewanee, the question they all asked was,

"Why did you stay?"

My response was, "I do not know."

Then someone retorted, "What do you mean, you do not know? Didn't Jesus tell his disciples, if they enter a town and the people did not welcome them, shake the dust off their feet and move on to another town?"

Our professor interjected, "There is a place for moving on, but it should not be impulsive. Rather it should follow some discernment; so, Joshua tell us about your discernment process."

There were several different things that contributed to my staying.

- I stayed to save face. I thought of the humiliation and embarrassment that would ensue following my departure from the parish, especially seeing that I came all the way from the Caribbean. I could just imagine hearing the critics asking, "Did he bite off more than he could chew?"
- I stayed because of the support and encouragement from my family and many parishioners. My ministry in the parish began two weeks before the solemn season of Lent. The challenges and sufferings I encountered then enabled me to identify with our Lord's passion and death. At the end of one of the services on Easter Sunday, while greeting the parishioners, a woman hugged me and said, "Thank you for coming to be our new rector."

Her embrace and words reminded me of Mary Magdalene's discourse with the risen Lord in the garden on the day of his Resurrection. That lady who thanked me ministered to me.

- I stayed because I had a family to support. I wanted to be a role model for my children, teaching them the virtues of perseverance.
- I stayed because of the spiritual strength I received from the daily office, prayers, meditation, and the Eucharist. I often resonated with a passage of scripture assigned for the daily reading. One day, for example, the morning prayer was about when Moses and the Israelites left Egypt (Exodus 17:1–7). They were in the wilderness. The wilderness experience was quite challenging, and the people were hungry and thirsty. They argued with Moses, saying, "Why did you bring us out of Egypt, to kill us and our children and our livestock with thirst?"

> Moses cried out to God. The Lord said,
> "Moses, go on ahead of the people, and take some of the elders of Israel with you; take in your hand the staff with which you struck the Nile, and go. I will be standing there in front of you on the rock at Horeb. Strike the rock, and water will come out of it so the people may drink" (Exodus 17:5).

Moses did as the Lord told him, and they got water to drink in the sight of the elders of Israel.

Those were words of encouragement for me that day. They spoke authentically. Stop complaining and murmuring, and go forward with the assurance that God is with me. I did and began to gradually embrace the task ahead of me.

Another lectionary reading that resonated with me was the Gospel for Refreshment Sunday in Lent. It was about the feeding of the multitude with the five loaves and two small fishes. I readily identified with the boy who offered up his meal to be shared with the community. I was moved by the four actions of our Lord. He took, he blessed, he broke, and he gave. These four actions are very present in the Eucharistic prayer. I meditated on these four actions, along with Eucharistic prayer:

> And here we offer and present unto thee, O Lord, ourselves, our souls, and bodies; to be a reasonable, holy, and living sacrifice unto thee; And although we are unworthy, through our manifold sins, to offer unto thee any sacrifice, yet we beseech thee to accept this our bounden duty and service, not weighing our merits, but pardoning our offences, through Jesus Christ Our Lord (BCP, pp. 337–38).

The most painful of the four actions is the "brokenness." No one likes to be broken. Yet it is only when the bread is broken that it can truly be shared with others. Jesus transformed the Jewish Passover meal, by referring to His brokenness on the cross, which anticipates His Resurrection. With this spiritual insight, I began to look at my sufferings and challenges as part of that brokenness. In this light, I identified with Henri Nouwen's book, *The Wounded Healer,* and began rereading it. That anonymous woman who embraced me on Easter Sunday and thanked me for coming to be their rector must have seen my wounds and saw hope for the healing of the community.

- I stayed because, like the Apostle Paul, "I was afflicted in every way, but not crushed; perplexed, but not driven to despair; persecuted, but not forsaken, struck down, but not destroyed" (2 Corinthians 4:4–9).
- I stayed because of the accumulated evidences of God's abiding presence that enabled my family and me to overcome these obstacles. They reinforced our commitment to the task ahead; with the affirmation, "We can do all these things through Christ who strengthens us'" (Philippians 4:13).
- I stayed because the alternatives were far worse. When many of Jesus's followers deserted him, Jesus asked the twelve disciples: "Do you want to leave too?"

Simon Peter answered him, "Lord, to whom shall we go? You have the words of eternal life. We have come to believe and to know that you are the Holy One of God" (John 6:67–69).
While there were alternatives, I did not consider them. Perhaps, I was not looking. I just wanted to bloom where I was planted.

- I stayed because my mother taught me there is a silver lining behind every dark cloud; that weeping endures for a night, but joy comes in the morning (Psalm 30:5).
- I stayed because in reading Paul's letter to the Romans, I found these words: "Don't quit in hard times, Pray all the harder" (Romans 12:12, Eugene Petersen's version, the Message).
- I stayed because somewhere I read these words: "Tough times can make you bitter or better." The choice is ours. I chose the better.
- I stayed because as Harriet Beecher Stowe says, "Never give up. For that is just the time the tide will turn."
- I stayed because I was stubborn, and I believed that God will vindicate me in due time.

- I stayed because I had the audacity to believe that God will assist me in changing the narrative.
- I stayed because, like Walter Brueggemann, I had a prophetic imagination. I visualized the church beyond its present circumstances and becoming a beacon in the community.
- I stayed because one day when I was at the breaking point, the lowest ebb, and about to give up, I turned to the passage of scripture assigned for that day in one of my daily meditations. It read:

A thorn was given me in the flesh, a messenger of Satan to torment me, To keep me from being too elated. Three times I appealed to the Lord about this, that it would leave me, but he said to me: "my grace is sufficient for you, for power is made perfect in weakness" so I will boast all the more gladly of my weakness, so that the power of Christ may dwell in me. Therefore, I am content with weakness, insults, hardships, persecutions and calamities for the sake of Christ, for whenever I am weak, then I am strong" (2 Corinthians 12:7–10).

I finished my meditation that morning with the singing of that ancient hymn:

> Oft in danger, oft in woe,
> onward, Christians, onward go.
> Bear the toil, maintain the strife.
> Strengthened with the bread of life.
>
> Onward, then, in battle move;
> more than conquerors ye shall prove.
> Though opposed by many a foe,
> Christian soldiers onward go.
> (Hymn A&M 291)

GETTING FIT

After much thought, prayer, and deliberation, I chose not to quit but to get fit. The story about St. Augustine's conversions is an interesting one. The young man's life was characterized by loose living and pursuit for knowledge. It is said that one day while he was outside, he heard a child singing, "Pick it up and read it; pick it up and read it." At first, he was uncertain about the meaning of the words. Subsequently, he thought the song could be a command from God to read the Holy Scripture. Consequently, he reached for the Bible, picked it up, opened it, and read the first passage he saw: "Not in carousing and drunkenness, not in sexual excess and lust, not in quarreling and jealousy. Rather, put on the Lord Jesus Christ and make no provision for the desires of the flesh" (Romans 13:13–14).

Those words pierced the heart of Augustine and led to his conversion.

In a comparable situation, I accidently came across a piece of junk mail advertising a seminar on conflict resolution. Intrigued by the topic, I immediately registered for the seminar, which was convened at a hotel at La Guardia Airport. Even though the seminar was not church oriented, I learned a lot. Specifically, there was a presentation on managing disappointment. The seminar was exactly what I needed. Stepping aside, time-out, using a new lens to look at the situation from a different perspective. Clement W. Lewis, in a sermon entitled "Managing Disappointment," said, "Whatever happens to you, seek to maintain an even temperament with respect to both anger and sorrow. Avoid becoming so emotional that you can't visualize the truths and complexities of a situation. Manage your disappointments and don't allow them to manage you. I will add, your disappointments may be the very seed bed where you are called to germinate, sprout, grow and bloom."

HOLY WEEK

It was now Holy Week, and I was meditating on our Lord's passion and death. I thought how he must have been disappointed with Judas, who betrayed him; the eleven disciples, who deserted him; and Peter, who vehemently denied him three times. Notwithstanding his disappointments, he never allowed those feelings to nullify his purpose in life. He never gave up on those who seemed to have seriously disappointed him. After his Resurrection, he entrusted the care of his flock, and his earthly mother, to them. I prayed that God would give me strength to look at my disappointments as temporary setbacks in the advent of a great comeback.

Maundy Thursday arrived, and I was alone in our makeshift garden of Gethsemane, observing an hour vigil. Here I contemplated Jesus's emotional prayer as he faced the impending crucifixion: "Father, if it is possible, let the cup pass away from me. Nevertheless, not my will but your will be done" (Luke 22:42).

His prayer became my prayer, a prayer of submission, a prayer for perseverance, endurance, courage, strength, and hope.

It was now Good Friday, and I had the solemn obligation to lead the congregation in a three-hour meditation on our Lord's last seven words from the cross, a meditation I have done previously. But this one was different. It spoke to the very core of my being. I was emotionally engaged, particularly to the words: "Father, forgive them, for they know not what they do" (Luke 23 3–4). I struggled with that Word. It became apparent to me that one cannot truly speak of suffering in the abstract. Suffering connotes a graphic image, and when the wound is fresh, as it was in my situation, it is even more painful. More painful even to forgive.

Years ago, I read of a psychologist named Lois who attended a seminar on Jungian dream interpretation. Carl Jung's grandson was one of the panelists. Members of the audience submitted dreams for the panel's interpretation. There was one dream that was very horrendous in which the dreamer was subjected to torture and cruelty by Nazi tormentors. Everyone wanted to hear what Jung's grandson would say regarding the dream. Much to their surprise, Jung asked the audience to stand and observe a moment of silence. Following the silence, the panel proceeded to the next question. Lois concluded, "There is in life a suffering so unspeakable, a vulnerability so extreme that it goes far beyond words, beyond explanations and even beyond healing. In the face of such suffering all we can do is bear witness, so no one need to suffer alone" (MaryAnn McKibben Dana, *Suffering, Forgiveness, Character, Hope. Journal for Preachers*, 2005).

As I meditated on the words, "Father, forgive them, for they know not what they do," I realized that it is of utmost importance that I forgive my trespassers, including the pharmacist who overmedicated our son. It is imperative that I do this so that I can effectively manage my disappointments. Forgiving the pharmacist was not easy. I suppose, too, it was not easy for our Lord to forgive those who were responsible for his death. One commentator said Jesus found it difficult to forgive his perpetrators, so he asked his Father to forgive them. Similarly, I remembered those who caused me pain and prayed, "Father, forgive them, for they know not what they do."

Yes, Enid and I forgave the pharmacist, to the point that we did not pursue a lawsuit. Coming from the Caribbean, we were not steeped in the American lawsuit culture. Initially, people encouraged us to take legal action. That we did, but we found it difficult to be praying to God to save our child's life and at the same time seeking revenge (although the lawsuit was not revenge, but rather seeking justice). Our primary concern was the well-being of our son. We focused our energy on that, surrendering the case to God, and the outcome was good. Justice is manifested in different ways; for us, it came in the saving of our child's life, and we were content with that. Today, thirty-four years later, we still have no regrets of going that route. We learned how to forgive and move on. Failure to forgive imprisons us and paralyzes us with the disappointments. Someone wisely said, "10 percent of life is what happens to us, and the other 90 percent is how we react to it."

So that Good Friday afternoon, April 5, 1985, we had a personal funeral service in which we buried our anguish and refused to be defined with the shroud of death. In the power of the anticipated risen Christ, we steadfastly pressed forward, cultivating endurance, character, and hope. That day, we came to understand part of what the Apostle Paul meant when he said,

"Suffering produces endurance, endurance produces character, character produces hope, and hope does not disappoint us" (Romans 5:3–5).

We also appreciated more Edward Caswall's hymn:

> Glory be to Jesus who in bitter pain
> poured for me the life blood
> from his sacred veins.
> (The 1982 Hymnal # 479)

DISCOVERING GLORY IN SUFFERING

It is one thing to recognize God's presence in times of joy, but when you experience that presence in your suffering, it is even more profound. As painful as such situations may be, they are wonderful opportunities to grow. That, my friend, is, blooming where you are planted. Friedrich Nietzsche, the German philosopher, said it so eloquently:
"That which does not kill us, makes us stronger."

In hindsight, Lent was the most appropriate time to begin my ministry at St. David's. The trials and tribulations I encountered helped me to identify with our Lord's passion.

In his epistle, James said, "Count it all joy, my brethren, when you meet various trials, for the testing of our faith produces steadfastness" (James 1:2–3).

There is usually a honeymoon period at the onset of a pastoral ministry. Mine was far from that. In fact, it was a nightmare filled with adversity, sufferings, tribulation, and pain. The soil was not the ideal one for planting, let alone blooming. No. There was hardly any soil, just a crack in the pavement, but enough to make a difference. Enough like the stable, when there was no room in the inn. Enough, like the five loaves and two fishes that fed the multitude. Enough, like the tiny mustard seed, which found a little soil in the pavement, germinated, sprouted, and bloomed. Enough to make a difference because God's power is made strong in weakness.

Yes, sufferings hurt. They are inconvenient, but I concur with Apostle Paul, who said they are designed not to defeat us but to make us stronger and wiser.

In his sermon "A Squirrel Crossing a Busy Street," King Duncan cited Sherwood Wirt's book *Jesus, Man of Joy* and gave a profound illustration of the positive role that pain can play. Wirt tells the story of James A. Garfield, who injured himself as a young boy while chopping wood. He was handicapped for a while. During his convalescence, he vowed to empower himself with a good education. He eventually was elected president of the United States of America. Note, it was while lying in bed in pain that he decided to change his direction in life.

John Rippons, in his hymn "How Firm a Foundation, Ye Saints of the Lord," says

> When through the deep waters I call thee to go,
> the rivers of woe shall not thee overflow.
> For I will be with thee, thy troubles to bless,
> and sanctify to thee thy deepest distress.

> When through the fiery trials thy pathway shall lie
> my grace, all sufficient, shall be thy supply.
> The flames shall not hurt thee; I only design
> thy cross to consume, and thy gold to refine.
> (The 1982 Hymnal # 636)

The suffering that produces endurance and steadfastness shaped my character and gave me hope in knowing that having survived those difficult times, I grew stronger, became less fretful, and was not anxious as I continued my ministry at St. David's.

FACING THE GOLIATH

I did not know I would come to this realization, but it was genuine. In hindsight, there was an advantage in me being in isolation on the onset of my ministry at St. David's. The Apostle Paul wrote several of his letters while he was imprisoned. Martin Luther King Jr. wrote a powerful letter from the Birmingham City Jail. Nelson Mandela used his time in prison to read and strategize the freedom of South Africans. Yes, prisons could be perceived as solitary confinement, but they can also be incubators, places where new ideas are conceived.

As previously stated, the patron saint for my home parish in Nevis and the parish in Antigua where I served was St. George. According to an ancient legend, George, a warrior in his travels, met a hermit in Libya, who informed him of a dragon that had long ravaged the country. Every day, a young girl was offered to the dragon as a sacrifice. Finally, the princess, the king's own daughter, was the only girl left for the dragon's prey. George, we are told, ambushed the dragon and killed it with his sword, saving the princess's life. The story is about courage and service. St. George's parishioners were exhorted to exemplify such virtues.

Seeing that I was called to be the new rector of St. David's Parish, it was incumbent on me to learn as much as possible about David of Wales, our patron saint. Information was scanty at that time, for I had not yet established my library. Consequently, I resorted to reading and meditating on the story of David in the Old Testament. 1 Samuel 17 records the story of David and Goliath, a very intriguing and familiar story. There are seven things I learned from this story that could apply to my situation:

First, David was chosen by God. Mention has already been made how Samuel, God's messenger, overlooked Jesse's older sons and anointed David to succeed Saul. We also saw the similarity between David's ascent to the throne and my election as rector of the parish. I was sought out. I did not seek the office. Jesus reminds us, "You did not choose me, but I chose you" (John 15:16). I was humbled to be elected and given such responsibility; no doubt, all eyes were on me.

Second, David trusted God. He was determined and had the confidence in God to believe that the Lord was on his side. David volunteered to challenge Goliath because he had a strong faith in God and himself. A dynamic combination of faith in God and faith in oneself can defeat the enemies that work against God's kingdom. The writer of the book of Hebrews reminds us that it is impossible to please God without faith (Hebrews 11:6). Jesus tells us, "If you have faith the size of a mustard seed, it would be large enough to uproot a mulberry tree" (Luke 17:6).

I was certainly aware of God's presence, but being human, I doubted at times. In those moments of trials, my single prayer was, "Lord, increase my faith."

Third, David recalled God's saving acts of deliverance in his life. He said, "The Lord who saved me from the paw of the lion and from the paw of the bear, will save me from the hand of the Philistine" (1 Samuel 17:37).

Reminiscing on the various obstacles that I overcame, I realized they were now stepping-stones for my new challenges.

The fourth virtue was courage. David was surely courageous to take on the giant. King Duncan, in his sermon "You Can Face Your Giant," described the scene in a powerful way when he said, "Visualize, if you can, a man who is a combination of Shaquille O'Neal and Arnold Schwarzenegger. Now make him three feet taller and cover him from head to foot in a sheet of metal.... Now visualize Macaulay Culkin, the star of the *Home Alone* movies."

David was no physical match for the Goliath, who looked at him disdainfully and said,

"Am I a dog that you come to me with sticks?... Come to me, and I will give your flesh to the birds of the air and the wild animals of the field" (1 Samuel 17:43–44).

I thought I was lacking in courage because I saw myself reserved and shy. Again, I reminisced and recalled the conversation I had with Philip Evelyn, my agricultural supervisor; when I said I was contemplating going to seminary, he responded with a simple question: "Are you sure?"

I replied, "Yes, I am."

Giving up a full scholarship to study agriculture took courage; choosing the unchartered waters of theology was adventurous. I thought Bishop Lindsay and his advisory board must have seen some trait of courage in me too, throwing me into the deep end of the pool, assigning me to a parish and exempting me from the usual curate tenure. I thought also that the Reverend Henson Jacobs must have seen some semblance of courage in me to think that I could take on the Goliath of St. David. Perhaps my colleagues saw something in me that I did not perceive.

I concluded with the opening words of that well-known psalm attributed to David: "The Lord is my Shepherd, I shall not want." (Psalm 23).

The fifth lesson I learned from the David and Goliath story was self-esteem. David, the little shepherd boy, volunteered to confront Goliath. King Saul tried to discourage him. Goliath was a giant, a professional soldier, and had much combat experience. King Saul said to David, "You are just a boy," and Goliath "has been a warrior from his youth."

David would not be intimidated. He was confident within himself. He was not lacking in self-esteem. I was certainly moved by this characteristic. Migrating from a developing country to assume a position in the United States could be intimidating. It is easy to become petrified by an inferiority complex. The remedy for this is self-esteem, faith in God, and faith in yourself. It took a lot of courage to leave your comfort zone and venture into the unknown.

The sixth lesson from the meditation is to be yourself. Avoid impersonating others. After King Saul reluctantly concurred with David, he suited him with his own armor in preparation for the battle. He placed a bronze helmet, which was too large, on David's little head. He dressed him with his protective coat, which was twice his size. Saul's sword was strapped over the suit of armor. It was too heavy, was cumbersome, and looked ludicrous.

David protested, "I cannot walk with these for I am not used to them" (1 Samuel 17:39). With that, he threw them aside.

What I took away from this is that you must be your own self. There is nothing wrong in mentoring and having someone as a guide and model; in the final analysis, you should be yourself. When I first came to the parish, someone referred me to a congregation in Brooklyn that was thriving at the time. I was asked to visit the congregation, converse with the priest, and use that congregation as a model for St. David's. Initially, I thought it was an excellent idea, but I found the priest reserved and guarded. I reflected on David trying to wear Saul's armor, which was too cumbersome for him. I decided to wear my own armor and be myself. As I meditated more on the armor outfit, Paul's letter to the Ephesians struck me:

> Finally, be strong in the Lord and in his mighty power. Put on the full armor of God so that you can take your stand against the devil's scheme. Stand firm then, with the belt of truth buckled around your waist, with the breastplate of righteousness in place, and with your feet fitted with the readiness that comes from the gospel of peace. In addition to all this, take up the shield of faith with which you can extinguish all the flaming arrows of the evil one. Take the helmet of salvation and the sword of the Spirit which is the word of God. (Ephesians 6:10–17)

The relevance of Paul's exhortation was indeed astounding. I reached for the hymnbook, looking for the song written by George Duffield, "Stand up, stand up for Jesus, Ye Soldiers of the Cross," and began singing it. The last two verses of the hymn made a tremendous impact on me:

> Stand up, stand for Jesus; stand in his strength alone;
> the arm of flesh will fail you, ye dare not trust your own.
> Put on the gospel armor, and watching unto prayer,
> when duty calls or danger, be never wanting there.

> Stand up, stand up for Jesus, the strife will not be long;
> this day, the noise of battle; the next the victor's song.
> To valiant hearts triumphant, a crown of life shall be;
> they with the king of glory shall reign eternally.
> (The 1982 Hymnal 561)

That night, I dreamt I saw my dad standing beside a lamp, as he usually did, singing away with his hymnbook. It was evident that I was not alone in the battle but was surrounded with a great cloud of witnesses. Reflecting on the dream, I recalled the story of a physical education teacher who received a letter from a former student. The class had to run a three-hundred-yard race, but Mark, the student, was reluctant because he always came in last. The teacher encouraged him, running alongside him in the last hundred yards, yelling, "Good job, Mark! Absolutely magnificent." Mark said his teacher was his best coach and the first person to encourage him. Subsequently, Mark went to college, even though one of his teachers told him he did not have the gift of writing. Notwithstanding that, Mark pursued his dream and remembered his coach, the physical education teacher. With perseverance, Mark reached his goal. The story of Goliath may not be a lesson on the power of positive thinking; rather, it is the story of God, who whispers to us that we can do it. God will be with us; with God's help, we will prevail.

Surely, it was God working through the cheerleaders, including my deceased father whispering to me,

be not afraid for God is with you. It is worth noting Goliath did not kill any Israelites. 1 Samuel 17:14 reads: "For forty days the Philistine came forward and took his stand, morning and evening."

The Israelites were just intimidated by the sight of the giant. Paralyzed with fear, they did nothing to confront the giant. The question was, who was brave enough to confront Goliath. It was David, Jesse's youngest son, the brave and courageous young man who successfully overpowered the giant with a small stone.

The seventh lesson: David did not confront Goliath in his own strength. Rather he confronted him in the name of God. Similarly, Peter and John healed the crippled begged not in their name, but in the name of Jesus (Acts 3). With this reflection, I immediately recalled the hymn, "Forth in Thy Name O Lord I Go."

Technically, having been called as the new rector, on my arrival in the parish, the supply priest should have vacated. This was not the case; he lingered on even though I had satisfied all immigration requirements and was issued a work permit. Meanwhile, my family waited in the Bronx like refugees. Who would ask the supply priest to leave? That was the question. I was not the one who hired him, and although I was called to be the new rector, I had not yet been officially installed.

St. Paul, writing to Philemon, made a passionate appeal to him to forgive his runaway slave Onesimus and receive him back as a brother in Christ. Paul said, "Though I am bold enough in Christ to command you to do your duty, yet I would rather appeal to you based on love" (Philemon 1:8–9).

For that same reason, I chose not to be the one to terminate the supply priest. Consequently, he lingered on for a while, until one day, Euclid Jordan and Stanley Gordon visited my family at my brother-in-law's home and informed us that they had told the supply priest to leave. It was now left to me to implement it. Still like St. Paul, I preferred Philemon to act out of his Christian calling rather than me enforcing it. That is precisely what happened. My family was again reunited, and what was once the stable and the war room became our new home.

I waited for another year before I was installed as the second rector. Interestingly, David was anointed three times as king but waited seven years before being crowned as king of Israel.

Bishop Henry Hucles, Suffragan Bishop of Long Island and Rev J. Mastine Nisbett May 17, 1986

CHAPTER 6

ON THE CUTTING EDGE

> I'm about to do something brand new. It's bursting
> out! Don't you see it? There it is! I'm making a road
> through the deserts, rivers in the backlands.
> Isaiah 43:18–19 The Message

In a previous chapter, "Living on the Edge," we observed how Jesus and others (myself included) lived on the edge. Walking a tightrope is risky and vulnerable. In Jesus's case, there is an interesting twist. Jesus lived on the edge and became the cutting edge, transforming those living on the edge: the lame, the prostitutes, the tax collectors, the outcasts, the lost sheep, indeed all humanity. Jesus became our bridge. Hence, we no longer have to walk on the tightrope by ourselves because Jesus, the bridge, is the Way, the Truth, and the Life that leads to God's kingdom. We no longer have to live on the edge, the tightrope, because God has made a way in the wilderness and provided rivers for our dry land.

In my first book, *A Journey to the Promised Land*, I chronicled the early history of St. David's Episcopal Church. With a humble beginning, the church was conceived and birthed in Mr. and Mrs. Robert Gnad's home, 116–31 230 Street, Cambria Heights. The first service was held at the Gnads' residence on February 11, 1940. Like Abraham and Sarah, who led an expedition into the land of Canaan, the Gnads led a crusade from St. Joseph's Episcopal Church, Queens Village, to start a new mission in

Bloom Wherever God Plants You

Cambria Heights. The adventure started with fourteen families, who were like nomads worshipping at three different locations on Linden Boulevard. On January 5, 1945, the congregation purchased two lots of land where the present edifice is located, 117–35 235th Street in Cambria Heights.

The sovereignty of God should not be overlooked here. While God was doing a new thing in Cambria Heights with the congregation, purchasing land to build a sanctuary, God was about to do a new thing in my family.

Shortly thereafter, my mother became pregnant with me, the future leader of St. David's, the one designated to lead in the building of the new edifice. This certainly resonated with the call of the prophet Jeremiah: "Before I formed you in the womb I knew you, and before you were born, I consecrated you. I appointed you a prophet to the nations" (Jeremiah 1:5).

The prophet Isaiah said, "See the former things have come to pass, and new things I now declare; before they spring forth I tell you of them" (Isaiah 42:9).

According to the church's annals, until early 1970, St. David suffered from a mentality best described by the refrain, "Poor Little St. David's," a mentality aided and abetted by a rapid succession of priests. Only a few stayed longer than two years, with an accompanying refrain emanating from some other voices referring to St. David's as "the church that should never have been built."

The rapid turnover of priests-in-charge came to an end when the late Rev. Leo Malania was installed as vicar. He and his lovely wife, Fae, and son, Dimitri, were a welcome addition to the St. David family. Father Malania was born in Tiflis, Russia, on May 21, 1911. He grew up in Canada, where he was educated, and later taught school prior to entering government service in the Ministry of External Affairs. He then joined the international staff of the United Nations and was the assistant to the first three secretary-generals, Trygve Lie, Dag Hammarskold, and U Thant. He ended this illustrious career as the UN's chief editor in December 1965. He was ordained a deacon in February 1965, and in June 1965, he graduated from the George F. Mercer Jr. Memorial School of Theology, Garden City, Long Island. As vicar of St. David's Mission Church, Father Malania was an outstanding leader. His generosity and love were boundless. As a theologian, he was profound. As a teacher, he was wise and intellectual.

These were quite some shoes to fill. It is only natural for someone to feel a sense of trepidation with the departure of a great leader and legend in the Episcopal Church. Father Malania was like Moses. He led the congregation to the threshold of the Promised Land, by helping them move from a mission to a parish status. Now with his demise, Joshua faced numerous challenges as a young leader who walked in the shadow of Moses. Stepping into his leadership role would make anyone's knees buckle. Joshua would have to be courageous and strong.

And in May 1986, that was precisely the charge the Reverend Dr. Kortright Davis delivered at my installation as the second rector of the parish. The Old Testament reading for that service was Joshua 1:1–9. Dr. Davis eloquently underscored the verses:

"As I was with Moses, so I will be with you; I will not fail you or forsake you. Be strong and courageous, for I shall put this people in possession of the land, I swore to their ancestors to give them.... I hereby command you. Be strong and courageous, do not be frightened or dismayed, for the Lord your God is with you wherever you go" (Joshua 1:59).

The preacher was profound and direct while I sat there and soaked it in. I paused and reflected personally on the significance of my name, Joshua.

Throughout biblical history, we note a recurring practice of a name change in certain people's lives. For example, Abram's name was changed to Abraham. Sarai's name was changed to Sarah. Simon's name was changed to Peter, and Saul was changed to Paul.

As a child, I grew up knowing my name as Mastine Samuel. These are the two names that were on my baptismal certificate. Mastine was a family name. It was the middle name of both my father and my eldest brother, Joseph. For me, though, Mastine was my first name, and I loved it because of its uniqueness. I associated Samuel with my spiritual formation. From early childhood, I loved the story of the calling of Samuel. James Drummond Burns's hymn, "Hush'd Was the Evening Hymn," was one of my favorites:

> O give me Samuel's ear!
> The open ear, O God!
> Alive too quick to hear
> each whisper of thy word.
> Like him to answer at thy call,
> and to obey thee first of all.

A & M Hymnal Book # 574

I was baptized when I was only nineteen days old. I resonated with the child Samuel, who was dedicated to God's temple at an early age. This was reinforced when I became an altar boy at the age of twelve. I tried to emulate the child Samuel, my namesake, throughout my discernment process to the ordained ministry.

It was not until I was eighteen and about to travel abroad for the first time that I discovered the name on my birth certificate was Joshua Mastine, not Mastine Joshua. Joshua, of course, was my paternal grandfather's name, a name that I struggled to embrace, since I only became aware of it when I was a teenager.

Installation of Rev J. Mastine Nisbett, 2nd rector of St. David's church. May 17, 1986.

Now, sitting at the feet of the distinguished theologian who eloquently expounded on Joshua's call to leadership, I was mesmerized and transfixed by this great leader. Dr. Davis's charge to me reminded me of Peter's declaration about Jesus at Caesarea Philippi. Jesus asked his disciples two questions: "Who do people say that the son of man is? but more importantly, who do you say that I am?"

Simon Peter answered him, "You are the Messiah; the son of the Living God."

And Jesus answered him, "Blessed are you, Simon son of Jonah! For flesh and blood has not revealed this to you, but my Father in heaven. And I tell you, you are Peter, and upon this rock will I build my church" (Matthew 16:13–18).

Dr. Davis had me so hypnotized that I felt he was no longer speaking about Joshua, the leader from the Old Testament. Rather, he was speaking to me. That is when I began to embrace my name, Joshua. It was like a name change, a metamorphosis. As Samuel, I received a general call into the Christian vocation. But now it was even more specific, for I was likened to Joshua to lead the people into the Promised Land.

James Merritt, in his sermon "Go for the Gold," said, "Joshua may have felt like a baseball player who was about to walk up to the plate with the bases loaded. It was the bottom of the ninth; his team is behind by two runs. Everything depended on him, and the coach called him back to the dugout and told him that the championship was on his shoulders."

I could have been easily intimidated by the task ahead, but I was emboldened by the preacher, who said that God wanted to remind Joshua that it is not the size of the man in the fight rather, it is the size of God in the man. God reassured Joshua that he would be blessed, just as Moses was.

As Joshua, the new leader stood on the threshold of a new beginning. God gave him two simple instructions: Joshua was told to "arise" and "go over the Jordan" (Joshua 1:2). "Arise": This is what you need to do right now. That is living in the present and recognizing God's presence in the here and now.

Arise. One gets the picture of Joshua probably sitting, or lying down, resting on his laurels, just marking time. He was probably speculating, certainly grieving over the death of Moses and still living in the past. It is in that setting that he hears the command to arise.

John Wooden, the former head coach at UCLA who won more national championships than any basketball coach in history, said that his father taught him one basic principle: "Don't whine, don't complain, don't make excuses.... Do the best you can" (cited by James Merritt's sermon, "Use It or Lose It").

The call to rise was very much germane to the congregation and myself. Our marriage got off to a rocky start; we were living on the edge. Now that the turbulence subsided, and our seat belts were unfastened, the commander-in-chief summoned us to arise. Borrowing a line from the prophet Isaiah,

"Arise and shine for your light has come, for the glory of the Lord rises to shine on you" (Isaiah 60:1).

With an erect posture and having now risen, we hear the next command:

"Go over into the Jordan." Here we not only recognize God in the present but are assured of his continued presence in the future. James Merritt puts it rather nicely when he said,

"What God tells you to do today is always preparing you for what God wants you to do tomorrow" (Merritt, "Going for the Gold").

The preacher insisted that the battle has already been won. "You are already victorious," he said, citing Joshua 1–3: "Every place that the sole of your foot will tread upon, I have given you, as I said to Moses."

Observe, God did not say, "I will give"; rather, the text stated, "I have given." In other words, God says victory is not a goal one strives for, but a gift you already have. Claim your victory then, he said. J. Miller, commenting on this verse, said, "It is not so much a mountain you are trying to climb, it is a peak you have already reached" (Miller, "Going for the Gold").

Apostle Paul witnessed to this victory when he said, "But thanks be to God, who gives us the victory through our Lord Jesus Christ" (1 Corinthians 15:57).

Miller summed it up nicely, saying, "It is sad to say, but for too many Christians, victory is a check uncashed" (Miller, "Going for the Gold").

"No one shall be able to stand against you all the days of your life" (Joshua 1:5a). A remarkable promise. Joshua will have a formidable force with which to combat his enemies. He would be like superman, immovable, triumphing over his enemies. Frances Ridley Havergal, the hymn writer, said it best:

> Fierce may be the conflict,
> strong may be the foe,
> but the king's own army
> none can overthrow.
> Round His standard ranging
> victory is secure,
> for His truth, unchanging,
> makes the triumph sure.
>
> A & M Hymnal Book. 683

"As I was with Moses, so I will be with you. I will not leave you nor forsake you" (Joshua 1:5–6). Both Joshua and Israel needed to understand that God was the most important factor, not Moses. Someone rightly said, "When a man becomes a monument, the movement will die." As with Moses, God promised Joshua that he would not leave him. So, too, Jesus promised his disciples and us, "Lo I am with you always, even to the end of the world" (Matthew 28:20).

In his charge, the preacher reminded me about the importance of meditating upon the word of God. Joshua was instructed to feast upon the word of God: "This book of the law shall not depart out of our mouth; you shall meditate on it day and night so that you may be careful to act in accordance with all that is written in it" (Joshua 1:8).

God's last words to Joshua were, "I hereby command you: be strong and courageous, do not be frightened or dismayed, for the Lord your God is with you, wherever you go" (Joshua 1:9).

Dr. Davis emphasized that there will be no real victory without the study of God's Holy Word. You must be a student of the Bible; read it, mark it, learn it, and inwardly digest it. Only then will you be victorious in the work God has called you to.

This was God's command to Joshua. He was responsible for seeing the mission from start to finish. God demanded a firm commitment from him. I realized that both the congregation and I were making a commitment to serve God's kingdom here on earth.

At the end of the service, I had some ambivalence. Excited, yes, but with some apprehension. The saving grace was Joshua 1:3: "Every place that the sole of your foot will tread upon, I have given you."

The battle has already been won. Is not this what salvation is all about? Jesus Christ, through his death and glorious resurrection, has won the battle on our behalf. All we need to do is to claim it. Of course, I was fully aware that there would be challenges. With the assurance that the battle has already been won and with the perpetual presence of God, I therefore committed myself to the task of the ending and new beginning of my ministry; Dr. Davis summed up his sermon with this hymn:

> Finish then thy new Creation.
> Pure and spotless let us be;
> let us see thy great salvation,
> perfectly restored in thee.
>
> Change from glory into glory
> till in heaven we take our place.
> Till we cast our crowns before thee,
> lost in wonder, love and praise.
>
> A & M Hymnal Book # 520

There are two things the service of institution did for me and the congregation. Personally, it helped me to embrace my name Joshua. Reminiscing on it now, I wonder whose idea it was to give me that name. Was it my paternal grandfather who was the sexton and lay reader of my home church for about forty years? Whoever was responsible was probably inspired to believe the hymn writer who wrote: "God is working his purpose out as year succeeds to year."

The second thing I took away from the service of institution was the acknowledgment of the transforming power of God. He was transforming us from living on the edge, to becoming a church on the cutting edge. The congregation that lived on the edge, with priests coming through a revolving door, was about to have some stability. That which was described as "Poor little St. David's; the church that should not have been built; the little church on the triangle," was about to be transformed into "a church on the cutting edge."

The psalmist said, "You spread a table before me in the presence of those who trouble me. You have anointed my head with oil, and the cup is running over. Surely your goodness and mercy shall follow me all the days of my life; and I will dwell in the house of the lord forever" (Psalm 23:5–6).

It is in this context that we understand the God who transplants us from living on the edge to becoming the cutting edge is constantly giving us commands and demanding that we bloom where God has planted us.

> Blessed are those who trust in the Lord,
> Who trust is in the Lord,
> They shall be like a tree planted by water,
> Sending out its roots by the stream
> It shall not fear when heat comes,
> And its leaves shall stay green
> In the year of drought, it is not anxious
> And it does not cease to bear fruit. (Jeremiah 17:6–7)

Our Sunday services should empower, energize, and equip us for ministry during the week. Similarly, the parish and I were emboldened with the celebration of the new ministry. Like the biblical Joshua, we were given our marching orders from our Commander-in-Chief, Jesus Christ.

Someone said Jesus only makes two types of statements: commands and demands. What demands does Jesus makes of us? Simply put: fulfil this mission:

"Go make disciples of all nations, baptizing them in the name of the Father and the Son and of the Holy Spirit, and teaching them to obey everything that I have commanded you" (Matthew 28:19–20).

Indeed, the church does not have a mission of its own. We take our mission from Jesus Christ, who first called us into ministry. "You have not chosen me, but I have chosen you, and ordained you, that you should go and bring forth fruit" (John 15:16).

In other words, we are called to advance Christ's mission.

Reference has already been made to my first sermon preached in the parish on February 10, 1985, exactly forty-five years after the founding of the parish. I chose Luke 4:18–19 for the occasion, though not part of the Sunday's lectionary. Expounding on the text, I stopped short of verse 19: "To proclaim the year of our Lord's favor," and verse 21: "Today, this scripture has been fulfilled in our hearing."

Now, thirty-four years later, I would like to revisit two statements from the text.

1. "To proclaim the year of our Lord's favor."
2. "Today, this scripture is fulfilled in your hearing."

To that end, let me chronicle the events in the life of the congregation:

- **February 11, 1940.** Founder Day. The first service of the new mission.
- **January 5, 1945.** Congregation purchased land at 117–35 235th Cambria Heights.
- **September 10, 1946.** The date of my birth.
- **September 10, 1949 (my third birthday).** Laying of cornerstone on the first edifice, St. David's, 117–35 235th Street, Cambria Heights.
- **February 10, 1985.** My first Sunday as the second rector in the parish, exactly forty-five years after the founding of the parish and forty years after the purchase of the land on which the church building is located.
- **November 24, 1949.** Thanksgiving Day. The parish hall was consecrated and dedicated. Forty years later, 1989, building plans for the new building were finalized.
- **March 24, 1990.** The eve of the Feast of Annunciation (nine months before the celebration of Christ's birth; St. David's announcement). Ground-breaking ceremony for the new edifice. This was the jubilee year of the parish, the fiftieth anniversary of the founding of the parish.

- ❖ **April 11, 1991.** Bishop Walker and I laid the cornerstone for the new edifice.
- ❖ **June 20, 1992.** Consecration and dedication of the new building.

This timetable should not be overlooked. In the Old Testament, the number 40 is very pervasive and important in the fulfillment of promises. For example:

- ➢ The rain in Noah's day fell for forty days and nights (Genesis 7:4).
- ➢ Israel ate manna for forty years (Exodus 16:35).
- ➢ Moses was with God on the mountain for forty days and nights (Exodus 24:18).
- ➢ Moses led Israel from Egypt at age eighty (2 times 40), and after forty years in the wilderness, he died at age 120 (3 times 40; Deuteronomy 34:7).
- ➢ The spies searched the land of Canaan for forty days (Numbers 13:25).
- ➢ Forty stripes were the maximum whipping penalty (Deuteronomy 25:3).
- ➢ God allowed the land to rest for forty years (Judges 5:31).
- ➢ Abdon (a judge in Israel) had forty sons (Judges 12:14).
- ➢ Eli judged Israel for forty years (1 Samuel 4:18).
- ➢ Goliath presented himself to Israel for forty days (1 Samuel 17:16).
- ➢ Saul reigned over Israel for forty years (Acts 13:21).
- ➢ David reigned for forty years (2 Samuel 5:4).
- ➢ The Holy place of the temple was forty cubits long (1 Kings 6:17).
- ➢ Elijah had one meal that gave him strength for forty days (1 Kings 19:8).
- ➢ Ezekiel bore the iniquity of the house of Judah for forty days (Ezekiel 4:6.)
- ➢ God gave Nineveh forty days to repent (Jonah 3:4).
- ➢ Jesus fasted forty days and nights (Matthew 4:2).
- ➢ Jesus remained on earth forty days after the Resurrection (Acts 1:3).

I could go on and on, but I think these examples should suffice for now. Clearly, the number 40 seems to be used by God to represent a period of testing or judgment, as the length of time necessary to accomplish some major part of God's plan in dealing with various phases of humanity. In this light, St. David's time line can be viewed as part of God's time line. Therefore, perhaps it was justifiable to add that statement, "Today's scripture has been fulfilled in our hearing." However, it should not be misunderstood as to who does the fulfilling. God, and God alone, directs the course of history. Therefore, our story is always a part of the larger story. In fact, we do not have a story; it is God's story. We are God's missionaries, deployed to fulfil his mission.

There are two meanings associated with the theme, Year of the Lord's Favor. First, it is a clear reference to the fact that the time for punishment for sins was over and through repentance, the people are now returned into favor with God. For example:

> If my people who are called by my name
> humble themselves, and pray, seek my face
> and turn from their wicked ways, then
> I will hear from heaven and will
> forgive their sin and heal their land. (2 Chronicles 7:14)

> The second meaning comes from Leviticus 25:
> You shall consecrate the fiftieth year and proclaim a release of the land to all inhabitants. It shall be a jubilee for you, and each of you shall return to his own property, and each of you shall return to his family. You shall have the fiftieth year as a Jubilee; you shall not sow, nor reap its after growth, nor gather in from the untrimmed vines. For it is a Jubilee, it shall be holy to you (Leviticus 25:10–17).

The Jubilee was a time of restoration and refreshment for the land and for the people.

The parish of St. David's was organized in February 1940. The eve of the Feast of Annunciation, March 24, 1990, was the day the parish broke ground for the new sanctuary. This was nothing short of restoration and refreshment for a congregation that struggled for fifty years; first wandering like nomads in the storefront buildings on Linden Boulevard, and then settling in its present location on 235th Street Cambria Heights. The congregation with a rapid turnover of clergy was nicknamed "the little church on the triangle." The church should not have been built. But now in its Jubilee year, there was a great announcement with the breaking of ground for a new building. Was not this part of the Lord's favor, a time of restoration for a struggling congregation?

There is another salient point that should not be overlooked, and that is the year of the Lord's favor. The Jubilee as it relates to blacks: I need not go into any great details about the plight and suffering of blacks in our society. Cambria Heights was not immune to the racial segregation that plagued our country. A more detailed account can be found in my book, *A Journey to the Promised Land*. Let us not forget that blacks were dehumanized and regarded as property of their masters. For the most part, the whites were convinced that blacks, whether slave or free, were not humans and had no souls. Accordingly, they were unworthy and incapable of entering the Kingdom of God. I marvel because while it was a white congregation that originally planted the church in the neighborhood, it was the black congregation, who initially had no status in the church, whom God chose to be the builders of the new edifice.

"Once you were not a people, but now you are God's people. Once you had not received mercy, but now you have received mercy" (1 Peter 2:10).

Of course, what the author of 1 Peter had in mind when he wrote the letter was to point out who we were before Christ came and who we became after we were adopted as children of God's family. The text resonates with the spiritual journey of the black congregation. The Civil Rights movement of the 1960s became a watershed period in our country. Blacks began to emerge from exile. Those who migrated into Cambria Heights and its immediate surroundings were gradually evolving into the middle class. They took pride in taking care of themselves and their new homes. In this way, they were unlike the Israelites who returned from the Babylonian exile.

The returnees from the Babylonian exile were somewhat impoverished and depressed with the conditions of their homeland and the ruins of the temple. The Israelites chose to focus primarily on the building of their personal homes. Restoring the temple was not on their radar. Hence, they procrastinated on the temple's restoration. It is in this setting that the prophet Haggai emerged, with an exclusive word from God to the Israelites to prioritize God in their life. They were not concerned with the restoration of the temple.

The people procrastinated. They argued with Haggai, saying it was not the right time to rebuild the temple, while at the same time, they were living in new elaborate houses. Shortly after that, God spoke to the people through the prophet: "How is it that it's the right time for you to live in your fine new homes while the home, God's Temple is in ruins?" (Haggai 1:2–4 the Message). The prophet exhorted Zerubbabel, the governor, and Joshua the High Priest, son of Jehozadat (not Moses's successor), to get their priorities right and rebuild God's temple. Within three and a half months, the reconstruction of the temple had begun.

I was blessed with a responsive congregation who not only took pride in their new homes but responded enthusiastically to the building of a new house of worship. This should not be taken lightly, especially given the dark period of the history of blacks in the Episcopal Church and the nation. The building and dedication of the new edifice was nothing short of a Jubilee celebration. The blacks, primarily of West Indian origin, demonstrated that they too were part of God's favor.

"Once you were not a people, but now you are God's people" (1 Peter 2:10 Eugene Peterson the Message).

> But you are the ones chosen by God, chosen for the high calling of priestly work, chosen to be a holy people, God's instruments to do His work and speak out for him, to tell others of the night-and-day difference he made you—from nothing to something; from rejected to accepted. (1 Peter 2:9–10)

As for the blacks, they, too, bloomed where they were planted. They soared like eagles once their wings were unencumbered, although beset by many trials and tribulations. They not only bought their new houses, but they built a new house of worship in the neighborhood from which they were once excluded. That was Jubilee. It was the year of the Lord's favor.

St. David's continues to be on the cutting edge, so much so that we participated with the Church Pension Group (CPG) in producing a video promoting the work of the CPG. The video was recorded at St. David's and was presented at the 79th General Convention of the Episcopal Church in Austin, Texas, July 2018.

> "Poor little St. David's. The church that should not have been built. The little church on the triangle, on the cutting edge."

CHAPTER 7

COWORKERS WITH GOD

On May 9, 1984, I was interviewed by St. David's Episcopal Church Search Committee for the position of rector. They made it abundantly clear that the erection of a new building was a top priority of the parish. Although it was not stated, I thought it was somewhat implied that the prospective candidate should have some knowledge in church architecture or construction. I still believe I was the least qualified in these two areas, for craftmanship was not part of my gifts. Nevertheless, this was the very place where I was transplanted and expected to bloom. I love the Message translation of Ecclesiastes 11:4–6:

> Don't sit there watching the wind. Don't stare at the clouds. Get on with your life. Just as you will never understand the mystery of life forming in a pregnant woman, so you will never understand the mystery at work in all that God does. Go to work in the morning and stick to it until evening without watching the clock. You will never know from moment to moment how your work will turn out in the end.

"God always uses imperfect people in imperfect situations to accomplish his will" (Rick Warren, *The Purpose-Driven Church*, p. 38).

I was transplanted from the tropical island of Antigua, basking in approximately 85 degrees all year round and then was suddenly plunged into what seemed like a deep freeze, with bone-chilling temperatures of approximately 10 degrees, and submerged in about a foot of snow in New York City. It was indeed shocking and challenging. Additionally, the general temperature of the congregation was neither hot nor cold. At best, it was lukewarm. It felt like a plant uprooted from a rich fertile soil that immediately goes into shock, causing its leaves to wither and fade. The plant droops and remains in that condition for a week or two, adjusting to its unfamiliar environment. After several days, new buds appear: the resurgence of hope. This was the pivotal point of my ministry.

Not long after I arrived in the parish, the Building Committee, which was temporarily put on hold, was revived. I must admit that I was at a loss during those initial meetings. Frustration was beginning to take root, and I began to wonder why God chose me for this task. I was no builder. I was not equipped for this job. Then the Lord spoke to me through the words of the psalmist: "Do not fret yourself" (Psalm 37:1).

> Why are you so full of heaviness, O my soul? And why are you so disquieted within me? Put your trust in God, for I will give to him who is the help of my countenance, and my god. (Psalm 42:6–7)

Then came some reassuring words:

> Did not I transplant you from Prospect Estate in Nevis and plant you in my vineyard? Was it not I who transplanted you from Nevis to the United Theological College in Jamaica? Who was it that transplanted you from Jamaica to Antigua? And now, I have transplanted you from Antigua to New York City to transfer my people from one building to another. As I was with you in the past, so I am with you even now. And I will be with you in the future.

The stated purpose for the building expansion was to grow the church. It dawned on me that we do not grow the church with programs and projects. In fact, we have no control over the growth of the church. That is not our prerogative. That is God's domain.

From my agricultural background, I recalled the mystery of the seed. Science will find it difficult to explain why a dormant seed can produce life when buried in the soil. What we do know is that once a seed makes contact with the soil, something within the seed starts to move and change. This causes the outer casing to give and changes the whole chemistry of the seed, thereby enabling it to produce life. Leonard Sweet maintains this is precisely what happens when a Christian is nourished by the Holy Spirit (Leonard Sweet, *Sermon: Solid Faith and Watered-Down Churches*).

While the Building Committee was focusing on the logistics, the important part of the equation was the role of the Holy Spirit in the entire project. The congregation was not embarking on an entirely new project; it was merely expanding on its existing facility. Gardeners prepare the soil, sow the seed, and water it, but they have no control over the mystery of the germination of the seed and the growth of the plant. So, too, the Building Committee must do its part, but it takes the work of the Holy Spirit to bring the plans into fruition. The plant can only grow, bloom, and bear fruit in a healthy environment. Addressing the factions in the church at Corinth, the Apostle Paul insisted that neither he nor Apollos was ultimately responsible for the growth of the church. He, Paul, simply planted, Apollos later watered and nurtured, but it was God, and God alone, who gave the increase. Ironically, the same was true when I arrived at St. David's. It was not the ideal setting for a building project, but this was precisely where I was transplanted and expected to grow.

Factions are divisive and destructive, and they often inhibit growth. Dissensions have their own magnetic power to draw even unlikely people together in an opportune time. For example, in St. Mark's Gospel, we learn that just after Jesus healed someone on the Sabbath Day, the Pharisees and the Herodians, two enemies of our Lord, conspired against him. It should be noted that the Pharisees and Herodians were mortal enemies among themselves.

In the Corinthian Church, sides were drawn, harsh words were exchanged, and the mission of the church came to a grinding halt. Paul's immediate goal was to restore order in the church so that the church could continue to be a beacon and light in the community.

St. David's building project was much bigger than previously thought. This was one cause for dissension among the congregants. Losing one or two members could have a crippling effect on the project. Like Corinth, order had to be restored at St. David's, and certain preliminary issues had to be dealt with.

The building project became a twofold mission: building up the Body of Christ and constructing a new church building. Using Paul's analogy of the various parts of the body to illustrate the Body of Christ (1 Corinthians 12), I launched a series of teachings with the theme, "We Are the Body of Christ." I wrote and circulated a supporting pamphlet. I also made a deliberate effort to get to know the congregants.

Proverbs 13:16 says, "Every prudent man acts out of knowledge." To me, that meant I should endeavor to find out all I could about the neighborhood I was about to serve. No missionary to a foreign country can effectively minister to the people without first understanding their culture and context. It would be foolish to do otherwise. We do not have to agree with the culture, but we must understand it (Warren, p. 165). To do otherwise would be like the blind leading the blind. Cognizant of all this, I browsed through the Parish Profile but was still hungry. I went to the local library in search of relevant information about what was now becoming my new home. Unfortunately, there was not much to go on.

To get some help, I asked the librarian assistant, "How come there is not much literature on Cambria Heights?"

Her response was, "I am sorry, but that's all we have. Perhaps you can undertake a project to remedy the situation."

I don't know whether she said this in jest, but like Mary, Mother of the Lord, who often pondered things in her heart (Luke 2:19), I reflected on that challenge, and on March 8, 2011, my first book, *A Journey to the Promised Land*, was published. The book encompasses not only the history of St. David's Church but also the early history of Cambria Heights.

After the passage of time and much effort, I knew most of the congregants and was able to call them by their first name during the administration of Holy Communion. This was invaluable in bonding with the members, who were often surprised that I knew their names. I also learned this congregation was not much different from any other. Those families that first seem to be everybody's ideal may, in fact, be a blended family from painful divorces. Some parents were working very hard to meet their financial obligations. Many were encountering racial prejudice. Others had problems with an adolescent child who was using drugs. The baby boomers were sandwiched between caring for their aging parents and simultaneously caring for their own children. Then there were those who were trying to rebuild their lives after being devastated by some catastrophe, like the death of a loved one. Notwithstanding all this, these people took their faith seriously. Week after week, they came to worship to be nourished, to be energized, and to be strengthened to face the trials of the coming days. The author Frederick Buechner reminds us that we are always in a state of becoming, not just who we are but who we are becoming (or failing to become). In other words, we are always in a state of becoming; someone cleverly designed a T-shirt with these words: "Christian under Construction."

On a recent visit to Ghana, I observed many unfinished houses. Like the Caribbean, where many people build houses without financial loans from banks, they build in stages, according to their financial resources. At the completion of first floor, they take up residence in the unfinished building and subsequently address the next phase of the building. They dwell in the house even while it is being constructed.

"Christian under Construction" means that we are already in the process of being built, even while we are failing to become. God is the builder. We are loved and accepted by him. The Apostle Paul reminds us that our bodies are the Temple of the living God (*1Corinthians 6:19*). "God is a Spirit and they who worship him, should worship him in Spirit and in truth". Jesus told the Samaritan woman. (John 4:24). Just as we can live in an unfinished physical building, so too, the Christian is an unfinished work in progress. However, there are things we need to do to complete the process. As co-workers with God, we need to acknowledge the fact that there is some growth yet to be achieved. God loves us and accepts us as we are, so we ought to do likewise. In doing so, we will be able to remove the shame we experience because of our shortcomings. In the Christian Construction, we are always in a state of becoming. There is no place for complacency in the Christian life. All obstacles that inhibit growth must be removed so that we can live into our true potential. Failure to do this can be likened to a plant that has lost its essential "plantness". It loses its ability to produce, and to bloom, to bear fruit and to flourish. Even its identity becomes deformed. *(Leonard Sweet* "Solid Faith").

A good gardener knows the value of repotting a plant. The gardener knows that a small pot will stunt its growth. Repotting the plant allows its roots to spread; the plant grows taller, with stronger branches, and bearing much fruit. It is in this context that we understand the transplanting or repotting of St. David's family from its first edifice, which it had outgrown, to a more spacious yet modest building.

The spiritual house took precedent over the physical, and rightly so. Let us not forget that the early Christians convened in individual homes. Sometimes, there are larger number in an outdoor service. The service of institution for my rectorship was held outdoors, and for the past five summers, we have had outdoor services on the church's lawn. These services are well attended, exceeding the indoor capacity. We cannot minimize the importance of a physical building in the enhancement of worship. However, the psalmist reminds us "Unless the Lord builds the House, their labor is in vain who built it" (Psalm 127:1).

It is God who builds the church and invites us to be coworkers in the enterprise. Let us bear in mind that the worshiping of God cannot be limited to physical buildings. St. Paul reminds us, "God does not dwell in temples made with human hands" (Acts 17:2–4).

We are the temples of God. This makes each one of us a true church, which constitutes the Body of Christ.

THE CONSTRUCTION OF THE NEW EDIFICE

Now the second part of the mission is the construction of the church building. After a season sustained by prayers, faith, hope, patience, endurance, listening, reconciliation, and minimized tensions, an oasis was discovered, like that of a crack in the sidewalk.

I must say that much of the preliminary work for the building project was already in place at the time of my arrival. There was a parish survey regarding the proposed project, a stewardship campaign, and a building fund of about thirty thousand dollars. There were also some preliminary drawings for the proposed building. It was the dream of the congregation, along with my esteemed predecessor, the late Leo Malania, to erect the new building. My role was to enable them to fulfill their dream. I am a fervent believer that wherever God guides, he provides. When God calls us to do anything, we are always equipped for the task.

As the new leader, my job was to check the pulse of the congregation, accept them where they were, and accompany them on their faith journey. This process is so important. Often when a new leader comes on board, the thinking is to dismantle everything of the past and make a completely new beginning. Of course, there are times when this is justified, but we must bear in mind that pastors come and go, but the faithful laity remain. They too have a vision. God works through them as well. No one has a monopoly on God's Spirit. In fact, it was the Holy Spirit who enabled us to have a relatively smooth transition and continue our mission. We do not have to be original in everything, but we should at least be effective.

The congregation had a dream, and we collectively re-evaluated it. This is so vital in the planning stage. Too often, congregations get carried away with unrealistic dreams. Rick Warren in his book quotes Winston Churchill, who said, "We shape our buildings, and the they shape us" (Warren, p. 78).

The members of the Building Committee must restrain themselves from unrealistic building projects that exceed its current capacity to fund. Overbudgeting can cause a diversion of funds from actual ministry to pay for a mortgage. Should this diversion happen, it would be like the tail wagging the dog.

After much reassessment and prayers, I finally embraced the dream, like Joseph, the dreamer in the Old Testament. I was called to interpret the dream and share it with the congregation. The time for action had come. I was reminded of the time God told Joshua to stop praying about his failure and to get up and correct the problem (Joshua 7:10) There is a time to pray, a time to plan, and a time to act, and the time had come for us at St. David's to act.

This was a monumental task. Surely not one for cowards. In his first address to Parliament, Winston Churchill, prime minister of England, said he was putting politics aside and forming a national government that included all parties to wage war against Germany. He said he would tell he told his new ministers: "I have nothing to offer but blood, nd sweat" (May 13, 1940).

With the colossal task ahead of us, the Lord equipped us with an army, full of courage, and like that of Churchill's, whose goal was victory. Nothing to offer but blood, toil, tears, and sweat. Those words are surely demanding and may seem foolish, don't they? I recalled my supervisor, Philip Evelyn, thought I was crazy when I turned down a government scholarship to study agriculture. St. Paul, in his first letter to the Corinthians, said, "Our dedication to Christ makes us look like fools" (1 Corinthians 4:10 NT&T).

Apostle Paul also stated that "the wisdom of this world is foolishness with God. For it is written, He catches the wise in their craftiness" (1 Corinthians 3:19).

TEAM EFFORT

We plodded on, working laboriously on the task ahead as God's fools. Edward White, a former pastor who grew up in Boston, and quite naturally a fan of the Boston Red Sox and Boston Celtics, observed that the Red Sox seldom won the league championship because they never learned to play as a team. On the contrary, the Boston Celtics won the National Basketball Association Championship eleven out of thirteen years because they played as a team. There were no individual stars who stood out on the team. They were an extraordinarily well-balanced team (Richard Hasler, "How Things Grow").

One of the first things that Joshua did after he assumed leadership of the Israelites was to prepare his army for the invasion of the land. He commanded his officers to "prepare your provisions, for in three days you are to cross over Jordan to go take possession of the land that the Lord God gives you to possess" (Joshua 1:1).

Similarly, the Building Committee was reactivated shortly after I took up duties in the parish. As was noted earlier, the parish had plans for expanding its facilities even before my arrival. These plans were tentatively put on hold during the search for the new rector. Now the committee was prepared to move forward with plans to build the edifice.

The following were the members of the original Building Committee: Stanley Gordon (chair); Euclid Jordan (public relations); Bruce McLeod (resident architect); Emerson Spencer (civil engineer); Chester Brower (legal aid); Eugene Wilson (finance); other committee members were Ashford Clunie, Carlene Cumberbatch-Smith, Sylvester Fauconier, David Fleming, Karlene Gordon, Lloyd Parks, Valerie Philpotts, Garrick Reid, Lois Rodney, Louis Timmer, and Beverly Wilson. With the tenacity of the Building Committee and the generosity of the parishioners, we gradually advanced toward our goal. One of our greatest challenges was to mobilize the congregants to support the project financially. We are indebted to Stanley, Euclid, and Sylvester, who championed this cause. A wholistic approach to stewardship was emphasized. People are generally turned off whenever the subject of money is mentioned in churches. They often accuse the church of only being interested in their money. We were blessed to have the Reverend Dr. Nathan Wright as a stewardship consultant, who looked at stewardship from a wholistic point of view. We looked at the total person, their resources, and their relationship with God and their neighbor. We showed interest in their entire life. We ministered to them pastorally. A deliberate decision was made to downplay capital fundraising in favor of tithing. Capital fundraising is a one-shot deal, whereas tithing is ongoing, and if the church was going to have a mortgage, then tithing was the best route. When we began, the people were giving just about 2 percent of their earnings. We thought that asking the congregants to move from 2 to 10 percent would be too demanding. Consequently, we decided to start at 5 percent and then gradually move forward. This was well received. Many in leadership positions wrote affirmative statements supporting tithing.

Unfortunately, many of the recent converts to tithing relocated to sunny Florida or were called home to glory. Many of those who relocated continued in their faith journey. In a sense, we were their catechists, training them to be ready for their next mission. Even though we miss them and appropriately grieve over their relocation, we rejoice that we could transfer them not just as little seedlings, but as blooming plants. It should be noted many continued to support St. David's financially long after their exit.

As always, saying goodbye to longtime acquaintances and friends was painful. What kept us in balance was that the Lord was always sending new disciples into the vineyard. There was never a lull.

The stewardship appeal was a success (as indicated by the chart below):

1984	1985	1986	1987	1988	1989
66,018	127,752	130,763	149,655	186,304	263,600

This campaign was not unique to St. David's. The Diocese of Long Island at that time had many workshops educating parishes about the significance of tithing. Of all the parishes participating in this program, St. David's response was probably one of the most outstanding. This was validated by a telephone call from the Reverend Dr. Wright, the stewardship consultant. He was hospitalized at the time at Mary Immaculate Hospital in Jamaica, Queens. He had called from his bedside and said, "Mastine, I want you to go to St. James Episcopal Church on Capitol Hill in Washington DC."

"Who, me?" I asked. "What for?"

He said, "The doctor has placed me on bedrest, but I was scheduled to speak to the congregation on tithing."

"I am sorry to learn about your illness, but why me? Surely there are more competent people who can speak on the topic."

"Mastine, what your parishioners have done is remarkable. All you have to do is to tell your story."

I felt humbled and yet honored to be asked to represent the stewardship committee on behalf of Dr. Wright. With his coaching, I proceeded to Washington. The workshop went well. At its conclusion, one of the parishioners, a middle-aged Caucasian gentleman, gave me a short tour of the city. He was warm and friendly and seemed fairly educated.

"Father Nisbett, where are you from originally?"

"Nevis."

"Where is that? Never heard of that place."

I took a ten-dollar bill from my wallet and showed it to him. Pointing to the picture on the bill, I asked, "Do you know this individual?"

"Of course; he was the first Secretary of the Treasury, Alexander Hamilton."

"Do you know where he was born?"

"No, but I guess somewhere in the United States."

"He was born on the little Caribbean island of Nevis."

"You have to be joking."

"I kid you not."

"I have to check that out."

"Be my guest."

Cell phones and Google were not yet popular. A few days later, he called me and thanked me for the address on tithing and the history lesson on Alexander Hamilton.

That, indeed, was a teachable moment and underscored the theme, "Bloom where you are planted." A young man from the remote island of Nevis, following the footsteps of one of our founding fathers, blooming not only in Cambria Heights but in Washington DC as well. The incident reminds me of when Jesus was twelve years old and engaged in an intellectual discussion with doctors and lawyers in the temple, much to their amazement.

I recalled a conversation about a congregation certainly more affluent than St. David's, where it was stated, if they were to step up toward the tithe and were successful, they would not know what to do with the money. The congregants of St. David's knew exactly what the church would do with the money, so they gave generously and sacrificially. There were only about one hundred and fifty solid core members who initially supported the project. Within four years, we raised $651,582. The project generated enthusiasm, perhaps sometimes too much. At one time, we had four subcommittees of the Building Committee specifically charged to raise funds for the building project. Mindful of the text, "Zeal for your house will consume me," we suspended the subcommittees and formed one central Fundraising Committee. The church must constantly reassess itself and be mindful of the fact that it can destroy itself by the very effort it employs to expand it.

With all the noble effort we made, we still had to seek outside funding. First, we approached the Diocese of Long Island. We were told that it was not in any position to give loans or grants. We were directed to the

Episcopal Church Building Fund at 815 Second Avenue in Manhattan. From this source, we were able to obtain two small loans totaling $125,000. These loans were made to the parish via the Diocese of Long Island. Still, these sums were not adequate for the project.

Our next source of contact was the Bank of New York, a local commercial bank which we had done business with for several years. The bank was open to the enterprise, although most banks consider churches as poor clienteles for mortgages. Their rationale is if the church is not able to meet its commitments, what recourse would the bank have? Could it initiate a foreclosure on the building? How would that affect the bank's public reputation? If the bank repossessed the property, the question arises of who would purchase it? Certainly, there were more questions than answers. The uncertainty of a loan from the bank was even more precarious when it requested the Social Security number of the vestry members. This was an impasse. True, members gave generously. But to ask them to disclose their Social Security number and possibly risk all their assets would have been asking too much. In fact, the question was never even entertained. After all, the Episcopal Church is not a congregational church, wherein the church is owned and governed by the congregation. Rather, the center of authority lies in the Episcopate, which is the bishop. and each congregation is subjected to the governance of the Episcopate. Who then would risk all their financial possessions in the given situation?

On learning that the now-defunct Freedom National Bank was friendlier toward churches, we began exploring this avenue. Before we could make a formal request to the bank, we learned it was having financial struggles. Subsequently, it went bankrupt, and several of its clients lost part or all their savings. One of our sister churches, which had a similar building program such as ours, was a victim of the bank's demise.

We were really at an impasse. While we had raised $651,582 and had secured a loan of $125,000 from the Episcopal Building Fund, we were still hungry and in the wilderness. We needed another $450,000. Could God rain manna from above once more? Could the Lord provide water from the rocks, as he had done in the wilderness (Exodus 17:1–6)?

I recalled my favorite text: "'Behold the wood and the fire: Where is the lamb?' 'The Lord will provide.'" And surely, the Lord did provide. The telephone rang. It was the Reverend Heron Sam member of the board of trustees of the Diocese of Long Island.

"Mastine, how is the building project coming on?" he asked.

"We have made much progress," I told him. "The parish has raised $651,582 on its own, and we have secured two small loans totaling $125,000 from the Episcopal Building Fund. But we need half a million dollars."

"Wow, that's remarkable. How long did it take the parish to raise that amount of money?"

"About three and a half years."

"Wow. That's incredible. You all should be proud of yourselves. You are becoming a beacon in this diocese."

"Thank you. We are trying."

"Well, Mastine, the reason for my calling, I have some good news for you."

Immediately, a strange but delightful feeling came over me.

"Really?" I asked. "What's the good news?"

"The Board of Trustees for the Estate of the Diocese of Long Island has started a revolving fund to assist parishes like yours and St. Gabriel's building projects."

"Really!"

This was music not just to my ears but my whole being.

"Thank you ever so much for sharing this information with me. Please forgive me if I may seem to be presumptuous. You are not Heron, you are a herald of good tidings."

He laughed and said, "Now submit your application to the trustee."

I rushed from the office to the kitchen where Enid was. She must have seen the glow on my face and asked, "What are you so excited about?"

"Honey, I was just informed that the diocese is starting a fund to assist in building projects."

"That would be great, and our prayers would be answered."

"Thanks be to God."

I called Cy and Stanley and informed them of the good news. I could hear the jubilation in their voices. A formal application was immediately submitted to the board of trustees, and we were able to secure a loan of $450,000, which was the ceiling amount for the newly formed revolving fund. The $450,000 placed us in a stronger position. We now had a total of $1.2 million cash in hand to start the project. We had accumulated a significant sum of money to get started. We had improved on our history of giving and thereby made some long-term projections, which financial institutions could review when considering a loan or grant proposal for us.

With the completion of the drawings and our finances in place, we began entertaining bids from general contractors. First, we had three bids, but they all exceeded our budget. Consequently, we engaged the service of an independent contractor to provide us with a cost estimate of the project. We then had a second bidding with four participants. The firm of Hudson Development and Construction Corp. came closest to the cost estimate. Their initial bid was $1.6 million. It was finally reduced to $1.1 million. The firm agreed to loan us a sum not to exceed $200,000 in the event that we had a financial shortfall and were not able to complete the project. The term of the agreement was an interest rate not to exceed 12 percent, with loan duration of five years. Hudson Development was a Korean firm whose attorney was our state senator. He supported the project and promised to use his office to expedite the building permit, which we had not yet obtained. Members of the construction firm worshiped with us on one occasion. We note in the Old Testament story how Joshua sent spies into Jericho before he invaded the country. We did not use any spies, but evidently, spies were used on us, for I wonder in hindsight if the construction firm did not have an ulterior motive from our first contact with it.

Personally, my life was transformed because of the building project. I was introduced to Corporate America, including dealing with fraudulent contractors and ensuing lawsuits. Welcome to America.

Not long after the contract was signed, the firm reneged on the contract and held on to our $200,000 deposit, which we had to fight tooth and nail to recoup. This was a long, arduous legal battle that took an emotional toll on me. In a letter dated July 25, 1990, the attorney for the construction firm informed us that the company could no longer honor the contract because the church had failed to obtain the building permit. The construction firm was an imposter. It made great promises and dishonored them. Worst of all, it defrauded the church of some its resources.

We were caught in a great dilemma. Already we had received the loans from the Episcopal Church Building Fund, and the trustees of the Estate of the Diocese of Long Island. Payments toward the former were being made. Thank God we were not yet billed by the Estate of the Diocese. Those were exceedingly stressful times.

How do you retrieve your funds from a fraudulent contractor?

How do you deal with a wooden fence that was erected as part of the project and now becoming an eyesore?

How do you answer the parishioners increasing concerns about the project?

How do you deal with the grumblings from the naysayers?

"I told you so. You bit off more than you can chew."

How do you account to your lenders about the status of the project?

How do you preserve the pregnancy and avoid the miscarriage?

Above all, how do you preserve your sanity?

Night after night, after Enid left for work, I paced my bedroom, asking myself, *Is this the way God runs the church, plagued with so much disappointments?*

First, we were rejected on our arrival. There was no room in the inn, the rectory, for my family. Second, we almost lost our son, and now, we were plagued with a fraudulent contractor. When would it be over? Those were truly dark days in my life.

I wondered then whether the bishop's prophetic words at the groundbreaking ceremony had come to pass: "Anyone who thinks of building in New York City has to be crazy."

One night, I prayed, "Lord I am stuck! I don't know what to do. I am surrounded by enemies. What should I do? How long will it be? How long, Lord, will you forget us?"

Then I recalled my favorite text: "'Behold the wood and the fire: Where is the lamb?' 'The Lord will provide.'" I thought of the many obstacles I had overcome with God's help. Acknowledging the divine providence, I said, "God, are you still listening? Can you hear me? What are you up to now? Can I cooperate with you, or should I get out of the way?"

Father Nisbett perplexed over the fraudulent contractor's behavior.

I remembered the charge given to me at the service of institution by Dr. Davis: "Be strong and courageous, every place that the sole of your foot will tread upon I have given to you as I promised to Moses" (Joshua 1:2–6).

Nine long suffering months, like a pregnant woman. Nine long months of an extraordinary germination, when the seed remains in incubation in the underground before a new plant sprouts.

The words of our Lord came to me: "Except a grain of wheat falls into the ground and dies, it cannot bear fruit" (John 12:24).

I must have died a thousand times during those long nine months of pregnancy. On March 24, 1990, on the eve of the Feast of the Annunciation, we celebrated the conception of the project with the ground-breaking ceremony. But after a brief period of celebration, the project's momentum stalled. The tree that we were nurturing was cut down to the stump.

Then came my favorite liturgical season of Advent. It is a season of hope and light during darkness. In 1976, the hope was manifested in the marriage of Enid and me. In 1984, it was revealed in my calling to be the second rector of St. David's. On Advent Sunday, 1990, the Old Testament lesson was Jeremiah 33:14–16; it was timely:

> The days are surely coming, says the LORD, when I will fulfil the promise I made to the house of Israel and the house of Judah. In those days and at that time I will cause a righteous Branch to spring up for David; and he shall execute justice and righteousness in the land. In those days Judah will be saved, and Jerusalem will live in safety. And this is the name by which it will be called: "The LORD is our righteousness."

The prophet's message of hope and restoration came to us on December 13, 1990, when the CEO of Hudson confessed that he had stolen our money and agreed to repay the full deposit of $200,000, plus $25,000 for damages. Their payment was in the form of postdated checks from Moishe, a Jewish firm, made payable to Hudson for the benefit of St. David's. The church was reluctant to accept Moishe's check as part of the agreement, but it was the best offer on the table.

Hudson's confession of judgment was like a little branch springing up from what looked like a dead stump. Or as Maya Angelou writes, "Just like moons and like suns, with certainty of tides, just like hopes springing high, still I'll rise."

One cannot bloom where one is planted until the process of germination is completed. For us, it was a period of nine months. It was a ray of hope in our overwhelming darkness. The tree that was cut down and appeared like a dead stump was about to spring once more. The following Sunday was the second Sunday of Advent; the message was further amplified with this hymn:

THE SONG OF ZECHARIAH, *BENEDICTUS DOMINUS DEUS*

Blessed be the Lord, the God of Israel;
he has come to his people and set them free.
He has raised up for us a mighty savior,
born of the house of his servant David....
You, my child, shall be called the prophet of the Most High,
for you will go before the Lord to prepare his way,
to give his people knowledge of salvation
by the forgiveness of their sins.
In the tender compassion of our God
the dawn from on high shall break upon us,
to shine on those who dwell in darkness and the shadow of death,
and to guide our feet into the way of peace.

Yes, the child was not going to be aborted. The God of Israel visited Zechariah and Elizabeth in their old age; though she was once considered barren, she was about to give birth to a son. God had delivered them from their barrenness, as a sign of His deliverance of Israel from her enemies. That same faithful God was about to deliver St. David's from its enemies. "In the tender compassion of our God the dawn from on high shall break upon us, to shine on those who dwell in darkness and in the shadow of death, and to guide our feet into the way of peace."(Luke 1: 78-79)The dark gloomy cloud that overshadowed the project was beginning to lift.

With the advent message of hope and deliverance, congruent with the parish's dilemma, I began to ponder my personal life. Why does the Advent message play such a prominent part in my life? Then it dawned on me: I am an Advent child. Born on September 10, with all things being equal, I was conceived in the month of December, the Advent season. That was indeed an ah-ha moment. My mother never told me when I was conceived, nor did I ask her or have any reason to enquire. Now, in my seventy-second year, I am putting the pieces together, looking in the rearview mirror of my life. Reflecting on my past journey, the places I have been, the obstacles I have overcome, and the progress I have made makes it clear that it was God carrying me. Or as Frederick Buechner puts it, "If you want to know who you are, watch your feet. Because where your feet take you, that is who you are" (GoodReads).

The first set of checks from Moishe were honored by the bank, but thereafter, they were denied. We were duped on both sides. Then Hudson filed for bankruptcy. We were at an impasse. Elsewhere in the country, there were tensions growing between Koreans and African Americans. There was a call to boycott Korean merchants. Koreans were certainly not enjoying good publicity in the media. Then, of course, there was the famous Rodney King incident in Los Angeles; the anger directed at the Koreans resulted in riots. Some thought was given to join the picket line, but we decided against it for fear it would jeopardize our project. Instead, we worked quietly behind the scene.

With the advocacy of Assemblywoman Barbara Clarke, Euclid Jordan, the Bishop of Long Island, and my own intervention, we recovered $180,000 of the original deposit.

The demise of Hudson Development Construction Corporation reminds me of Psalm 1:4-5 "The wicked are like chaff that the wind drives away. Therefore, the wicked will not stand in the judgment, nor sinners in the congregation of the righteous; for the Lord watches over the righteous, but the way of the wicked will perish."

On the contrary, the psalmist said, "Happy are those who do not follow the advice of the wicked, or take the path that sinners tread, or sit in the seat of the scoffers, but their delight is in the law of the Lord, on his law they meditate day and night. They are like trees planted by the streams of water, which yield their fruit in its season, and the leaves do not wither. In all that they do they prosper" (Psalm 1: 1-3).

In the year 2000, the vestry took the suggestion of the bishop and agreed to bring closure to the case, since the company was no longer in existence. In addition, the monetary cost for pursuing justice was astronomical. In the book of Leviticus, there was a practice of forgiving outstanding debts in the Jubilee year. The year 2000 was observed by many as the Jubilee year and the year of debt forgiveness. By forgiving the balance of debt owed to us, we perpetuated the tradition of debt forgiveness during the Jubilee celebration. With this forgiveness, we felt more at peace with ourselves. The debt forgiveness symbolizes the meaningfulness of our forgiveness, the measure of our spirituality and the magnitude of our blooming where God had planted us.

Reflecting on that challenging experience with the Korean firm, I no longer regarded them as a foe but as a messenger to test us. Satan was sent to test Job. Likewise, Hudson Construction Firm was sent to test us. If the project had gone smoothly and without any adverse incidents, we might have been tempted to think that we did it on our own. Bad as the experience was, we were humbled and made more aware of God's providence. Moreover, we can concur with Apostle Paul, who said, "In everything give thanks" (1 Thessalonians 5:18).

Note the apostle did not say give thanks for everything, rather *in* everything. God is not the author of evil. He uses the evil to bring some good out of the evil, as the hymn writer puts it, "God moves in a mysterious way his wonders to perform."

When Hudson abandoned the project, we still lacked a building permit. This was finally obtained in November 1990 after much effort by the architect, Assemblywoman Barbara Clarke, and myself. I was a familiar face in the Building Department.

With no general contractor on board, we reopened the bidding process for the third time. This time, we elected to go the route of a construction manager. In this process, the subcontractors make a bid on the drawings, which is the actual cost of materials plus labor. The construction manager is paid a percentage of the construction cost every month. The manager's responsibility is to supervise the construction and finish the building within the bid price. If the manager successfully completes the project below the bid price, thereby providing a savings for the church, the manager receives a percentage of the savings as an additional bonus and as an incentive. With this approach, the church retained the role as the general contractor and saved us from initially outlaying any large amount of money. The only drawback was that having the church as general contractor placed more responsibilities on me, since the members of the Building Committee had full-time secular jobs.

Church Constructors Inc., a company specializing in church buildings, was employed to undertake the project. The proprietors of the firm were actively involved in their home church and were sensitive to the concerns and needs of our congregation. We worked well as a team.

On Saturday, May 11, 1991, the sun, which was hidden for several months behind the clouds of uncertainty, finally emerged. This was the day we began crossing the River Jordan, which took the form of excavating the land for construction.

Father Nisbett and Euclid Jordan

In Joshua 3:13, we read, "When the soles of the feet of the priests who bear the ark of the Lord, the Lord of all the earth, rest in the waters of the Jordan, the waters of the Jordan flowing from above shall be cut off; they shall stand in a single heap."

No doubt when the priests first walked on the newly created pathway that was formerly the river, they were tentative with their first steps. Those nervous first baby steps were critical. On the afternoon of the first day of the excavation, Bruce McCleod, our resident architect, visited the site. Bruce always gave his professional opinion; he was sometimes conservative. The committee highly respected his counsel. He told us that unfortunately, the excavation had damaged the foundation of the garage, which had to be removed.

I regretted this very much. Living at the rectory next door to the church's building had its advantages and disadvantages. Priests rarely get any time off. In addition to housing the car, the garage was used to obscure the presence of the priest on his day off or vacation. It was painful to see the garage go, but more importantly, the critical issue was the safety of the existing church building. Did the excavation compromise the foundation of the adjacent building? Was it safe to use?

An emergency meeting was planned for the following morning at 6 a.m., two hours before our first scheduled service that day. Stanley, Euclid, Emerson, Bruce, Pat Conquest (the construction manager, who travelled all the way from Pennsylvania), and I discussed the relevant issues.

The consensus was it was okay to use the building, but they all laid the final decision at my feet and said, "Father, it's your call."

I walked away briefly and thought, *What should I do?* I immediately recalled the miracle of the feeding of the multitude in the wilderness. If I send them away, they will faint. Jesus ordered the disciples to have the multitude sit down, and they were miraculously fed.

That Sunday, May 12, 1991, was Mother's Day. It was our second highest attendance service (Easter Sunday being the first). It was 6:30 a.m.

"Where can we send the multitude at this eleventh hour?"

Taking a leap of faith. I said, "We will have the service in the building."

This was perhaps the most critical decision I ever made. It was like Peter getting out of his boat to walk on water with our Lord. However, this was not just me walking on the water, but I was leading a group of faithful people to accompany me walking on the water with our Lord. That is radical trust in God.

More ushers were deployed that day, with additional responsibilities for the safety of the congregants. It was with mixed emotion that I presided at the Eucharist that morning. True, there was excitement we had come thus far. But the excitement was tempered with much apprehension. Any unusual sound could trigger off my alarm. I began the service with the reciting of the Travelers Psalm (Psalm 121):

> I lift up my eyes to the hills; from where is my help to come?
> My help comes from the LORD, the maker of heaven and earth.
> He will not let your foot to be moved: and he who watches over you will not fall asleep, Behold, he who keeps watch over Israel shall neither slumber nor sleep;

> The LORD himself watches over you; the LORD is your shade at your right hand,
> So that the sun shall not strike you by day, nor the moon by night.
> The LORD shall preserve you from all evil: it is he who shall keep you safe.
> The LORD shall watch over your going out and your coming in, from this time forth for evermore.

By the grace of God, we made it through the first service. The second was going to be the real test. It is more crowded, with many children in attendance. Provisions were made to have the Sunday school housed in the basement of the rectory next door. Now, imagine a home with three young boys. Every weekend, they had additional chores to tidy the basement for Sunday school. As parents, you know very well that much of that responsibility falls on you. There was a great sigh of relief when that second service was over. The soles of our feet had now touched the waters of Jordan.

Unlike the previous phase when we encountered obstacles, the construction phase went relatively smoothly. This was largely due to the invaluable support of the general congregation, the vestry, and the Building Committee, and especially Bruce McCleod and Emerson Spencer. During the construction phase, McCleod and Spencer took time off from their work on a regular basis for site meetings with the architect, the construction manager, and me.

Notwithstanding this, I must admit that the construction phase of the project was a burdensome one for my family. As the rectory was adjacent to the construction site, my wife, who worked nights as a nurse, wrestled daily with the construction noise as she tried to sleep. The construction put untold demands on me. In addition to my normal pastoral duties, I took on the responsibilities of general contractor. This meant meeting with disgruntled, unemployed workers who showed up at the job site, demanding jobs.

One day, I became very aware of my vulnerability. The construction manager, Pat Conquest, had not reported to the job site for several days. Later, I learned that he had gone to another job site, where the pastor had died suddenly of a heart attack. Euclid and Stanley probably saw the toll the building project was having on my family and insisted that we go away for a weekend. Such were the inconveniences and problems that confronted us during the construction phase. However, the satisfaction derived from the unfolding of the dream buoyed us to continue the journey.

As general contractor, I had the responsibility to hire and fire. One day, I caught a worker loading his truck with building materials and immediately fired him. I had learned my lesson from the fraudulent contractor. As the saying goes, "Once bitten, twice shy." The day after I fired the worker, the construction manager asked me to give the worker a second chance.

"Absolutely not," I said.

"Jesus said we should forgive our brothers and sisters seventy times seven," he retorted.

"He also drove the thieves out of the temple," I replied.

I wanted to use the firing of the pilferer as an example for the others. If you do not stand for something, you will surely fall for everything. At the job site, I used some of my supervisory skills I learned at Prospect Estate prior to my seminary training. I supposed I was overly vigilant because the plumbing subcontractor called me a black Jew. It is amazing how people think sometimes. They think the church should be passive, and then they take advantage of you, but Jesus said, "We should be wise like serpents but harmless as doves" (Matthew 10:16).

Yes, love can be tough at times. But there was a kinder, gentler side of me. An unskilled worker we shall name Tom was a frequent user of profane language. One day, I called Tom into my office and told him that his profanity was not going to be tolerated on this job.

"This is a holy site," I explained. "We are not constructing an ordinary building. We are building a house of worship."

Remorsefully and with tears in his eyes, Tom replied, "I am very sorry. I promise I'll do my best not to curse anymore. I can't afford to lose another job. I have a family to support."

"Why do you curse so much?" I asked.

He began sobbing and said, "Father, I was an altar boy for ten years, and I sang in the junior choir."

"Really! what happened?"

"Long story, Father. I got mixed up in bad company." He paused, weeping. "I ended up in prison, and there I took on that language."

"What did you do, to cause you to go to prison?"

"The cops arrested me because they found me with some marijuana. I feel like the prodigal son, and I want to reform my life."

We embraced each other for several minutes as he sobbed on my shoulder.

"Tom, I am going to help you."

"Would you, Father?"

"Yes, I am going to help you, but you have to help yourself as well."

"My wife would be happy for this."

I then prayed for him and blessed him. Two days later, I called Tom into my office and gave him a list of positive and negative words.

Within a week, there was a remarkable change in Tom's life. Not only did his vocabulary change, but his whole personality was transformed. Everyone noticed it. He became my informant on the job site and worked with us for several months. When we no longer had anything for him to do, I readily referred him to another construction firm. Several weeks later, Tom and his wife, Sue, visited me.

"We came to thank you for all you have done for us," Tom said. "You don't know how much I appreciate your kindness. I was in prison, and you visited me. I was hungry, and you fed me. I was naked, and you clothed me."

He then reached into his pocket and gave me an envelope with a hundred dollars for the building fund.

Sue then hugged me and said, "Thank you for saving our marriage."

That very day happened to be their fourth wedding anniversary. They renewed their vows in my office, and I pronounced a special blessing on them, after which they happily went away. They stayed in touch with me for many years.

Watering and nurturing Tom and Sue's plant was a remarkable story. Tom's biblical quote about being in prison was an affirmation for me. Remember, this was part of my inaugural address. I ministered to Tom and helped him to bloom where he was planted. He also ministered to me that day. He enlivened my hope.

The building was not completed, but we were already expanding our ministry. In the words of our Lord, "The fields were already white and ready for harvest" (John 4:35).

Even though the building was not completed, we were already doing mission work. You see, the building is not an end, in itself, but a means to the end.

The time came for the final phase of the crossing of the River Jordan. That took place on April 19, 1992. It was Easter Day, and our three services were held in the unfinished undercroft of the new building that was still under construction. We provided a temporary nave with space heaters. It was a glorious Easter. Worshiping in the undercroft was like entering the empty tomb. There we identified with the crucified and risen Christ. The previous struggles we encountered were like the crucifixion, but worshiping in the Holy Sepulcher, the undercroft was identifying with the risen Christ. It was truly our Passover made most evident in our ceremonial passage through the building. We entered the undercroft, our temporary nave, through a stairwell leading from the present narthex. To control the flow of congregants, we exited the undercroft through a circular stairwell on the other side of the building that landed on the second floor. No walls or roof were yet installed, only the concrete slab, which was the floor of the second level and the ceiling of the first level where we worshiped. Worshiping in the unfinished undercroft, which had once been just a hole in the ground, and then walking on a newly laid concrete slab above grade level was akin to the Israelites' experience of walking on dry land as they crossed the River Jordan.

We were well on our way to the finishing line when, early one morning a few weeks before the dedication of the sanctuary, the foreman rang the doorbell.

"Father, I have some sad news for you."

I immediately felt an adrenaline surge.

"What is the sad news?" I asked.

"Someone, or some individuals, attempted to set the building on fire."

"What are you talking about? You can't be serious."

I rushed to the building site.

"Oh, my God. Who did this? It must be someone out of his mind. How did the fire start?"

The foreman pointing to a garbage bag said, "Someone used a garbage bag that was left on the sidewalk of the property to set the roof on fire."

Suddenly, I felt chilly and began sneezing. I realized that I had left the house without my coat.

Hastening back to the rectory, I passed a neighbor, who said to me, "Pastor, I love your outfit."

I was still dressed in my pajamas. I returned to the rectory, just in time to stop another fire. In my rush to the job site, I forgot to turn off the burner on the stove. The kettle was destroyed, and the house was filled with smoke.

Two fires in one day.

Like all the hurdles we previously encountered, God was in the midst, for the garbage bag was not completely burned, and the timber on the roof was hardly scorched. It was like the burning bush, mentioned in Exodus 3. The bush burned but was not consumed. The God who enabled us to cross the River Jordan made a path from nowhere and intervened on our behalf, extinguishing the fire like a prompt firefighter. Only this time, there was no emergency call made. God, our protector, was watching over the building and saved it from being destroyed. The attempted sabotage was one more test we had to overcome. Of all the obstacles we experienced, the fire was symbolic of the furnace through which the gold that is being tested must pass. We are indeed a precious jewel when we do not succumb to our trials but are rather strengthened in our faith. We finally crossed over the Jordan River and went into the Promised Land. The River Jordan, of course, was one of the final crossings that the Israelites had to accomplish in their journey into the Promised Land.

Joshua 4:1 reads:

> When the entire nation has finished crossing over the Jordan, the Lord said to Joshua, "Select twelve men from the people, one from each tribe, and command them: Take twelve stones from here out of the middle of the Jordan, from the place where the priests' feet stood, carry them over with you, and lay them down in the place where you camp tonight so these stones shall be to the Israelites a memorial forever."

Following this noble tradition, we installed a marble stone on the floor of the narthex. On this stone, we inscribed the names of the following countries from which our parishioners originated:

Antigua, Bahamas, Barbados, Belize, Bermuda, Costa Rica, Cuba, Grenada, Guyana, Haiti, Jamaica, Montserrat, Panama,
St. Lucia. St. Kitts and Nevis, St. Vincent Trinidad and Tobago,
Turks and Caicos, United States, US Virgin Islands, U.S.S.R

It is important to note that the narthex joins the first and second edifice together. It is the bridge between the old and the new. After the floor had been completed, we successfully made the transition of transferring the altar from the old building to the new. The altar is symbolic of Christ's presence. It is like the Ark of the Old Testament that led the procession.

We have already observed the historical significance of Mt. Moriah, the place where Abraham was tested to sacrifice his son, Isaac. Likewise, we have noted some similarities between Jevon's near-death experience and that of Isaac, St. David's being the new Mt. Moriah. It is worth noting that in 990 BC, King David was instructed by God to erect an altar on the threshing floor of Araunah the Jebusite, which occupied the site. David purchased the land that later became the site of Solomon's Temple (2 Samuel 24:18–25; 1 Chronicles 21:18–26; 2 Chronicles 3:1). In keeping with this noble tradition, and part of the divine plan, we erected a house of worship at our Mt. Moriah.

And so, on Saturday, June 20, 1992, in a solemn and jubilant procession, we entered the Promised Land, singing the hymns "We Are Marching to Zion" and "Enter into Jerusalem; Let Us Go to God's House." The completion of the edifice was a great milestone in the parish's history. It made us proud, yet humble. It was a glorious day, one we had long prepared for. As I said earlier, it was on this occasion, while reflecting on my journey, that I became aware of the significance of my name, Joshua. It was Joshua who led the Israelites into the Promised Land. Now I was leading the congregation into our Promised Land.

Though King David was not the one chosen to build the temple, he nonetheless donated much of his personal resources toward its construction. Similarly, there were some who even though they were in transition to relocate and would not enjoy the full benefits of the new edifice, yet they did not withhold their resources. Here we are reminded of our Lord's teachings: "One sows, and another reaps. I sent you to reap that for which you did not labor. Others have labored and you have entered into their labor" (John 4:37–38). Those who sowed at St. David's will now reap in locations where they did not labor.

This means, the concept of "Bloom Where You Are Planted" must be expanded from the individual to the community, from the specific to the general. It is like Apostle Paul, who planted the church in Corinth. He did not stay to see it bloom. Apollos was the one who subsequently watered the plant, and the church community at Corinth bloomed.

Transitional membership has its advantages. It reduces the temptation to claim ownership of the building and idolize it. One plants, another waters, but it is God who gives the increase. Fruit bearing is God's work, not ours. Our job is to plant, fertilize, cultivate, and cooperate with God.

Currently, immigrants are going through some rough times politically. These days, it's almost an embarrassment to be an immigrant. Yet most of the congregants who were given the charge to build the house of worship were immigrants. They had nothing to be embarrassed about. They were new homeowners, teachers, nurses, doctors, lawyers, accountants, and so on. They all made a positive contribution to the society. Although they had their personal financial obligation with their new mortgage, yet they still contributed toward the new building. In April 2019, Myrna Guantlett Corby, an immigrant from Jamaica, West Indies, and parishioner for fifty years, commenting on the growth of the church, wrote,

"We all imagined that St. David's, formerly known as 'the little church on the triangle,' would always be the small brick church that was packed to capacity at Easter, with folks standing in the back by the organ and overflowing down to the small basement. We had no idea that St. David's could become what you, Father Nisbett, have made it, both in terms of the building and the congregation."

They bloomed where they were planted.

J. MASTINE NISBETT

The following are the words of a hymn I wrote that sums up the history of St. David's. The tune is Aurelia, "The Church Is One Foundation."

> Episcopalians traveled from Cambria Heights, New York
> to Joseph in Queens Village for all their worship needs.
> Donald, their Rector, saw the plight and asked Ms. Robert
> Gnad, who willingly shared her home to fourteen families.
>
> Like Israel of the old days nomadic was the church.
> Moving to three locations on Linden Blvd.
> Purchased a lot of prime land, they built a modest house.
> The new mission began to grow, in no uncertain terms.
>
> The Civil Rights new movement reached Cambria Heights at last.
> Led by Mayor William Durham, who crossed the picket lines.
> As blacks emerged, the whites fled. The mission was transformed.
> Thanks to Leo, the vicar, transition was complete.
>
> God raised your servant, Joshua, to carry on the work
> began by your own Moses to build a new building.
> The faithful gave and labored, accomplished that great task.
> In gratitude, we thank them for their unselfish deeds.
>
> Some planted, others watered, but God ensured its growth.
> May we never worship the building we have built
> build up the spiritual temple deep down within our hearts,
> build up the Body of Christ Lord for all eternity.

St. David's first edifice

St. David's second edifice

CHAPTER 8

NURTURING

It is now fifteen years after my arrival in the parish, eight years after the erection of the edifice, and one year after the satisfaction of the two mortgages from the Episcopal Church Building Fund; I began to contemplate whether the time had come for me to move on. I wrestled with this question at a Credo conference with the Reverend Michael Battle, who was my spiritual advisor. He said to me, "Mastine, you have two choices: stay or move on. If you stay, you should consider doing the doctorate in ministry as continuing education."

From the day we landed at John F. Kennedy Airport, I unintentionally abandoned my family. I already wrote about the physical separation of my family in the initial months. Once we were reunited and I was installed as the second rector, I became heavily immersed in the building project. We delivered a building within seven years, amidst all the problems, including a year of dormancy and in dealing with a fraudulent contractor. It is remarkable that we could accomplish such a feat in that short a time.

The eight years immediately following the erection of the building were financially stressful. We had a bigger plant to maintain, and we began servicing the third mortgage with the accumulated interest. It was a ten-year loan at a variable interest rate based on the current market. There was a time when we agonized over which bill to pay. Our mortgage payment, at one time, exceeded four thousand dollars per month. Then there were salaries, utilities, and so on. I recalled my favorite text: "'Behold the fire and the wood, but where is the lamb for a burnt offering?' Abraham said, 'The Lord himself will provide the lamb for a burnt offering, my son'" (Genesis 22:7–8 NRSV).

And the Lord surely did provide, so much so that we surprised ourselves by satisfying all three mortgages ahead of schedule.

Much credit should be given to Enid, who stayed at home with the children for three years while we acclimatized ourselves to our new environment. She did an incredible job in helping our children adjust to the new environment where they had been transplanted.

Discerning whether I should move on or stay was a thoughtful process. Three different times, I was asked to consider submitting my name to search committees as a candidate for rectorship. I was even approached by a diocesan bishop to consider the position of dean at his cathedral.

In weighing the pros and cons, I thought it was not wise to uproot my family at a time when we were just getting adjusted to our new environment. Personally, I was fifteen years older and had subjected my body to an awful lot. I needed to begin to take better care of myself. For fifteen years, I had labored with great restraint to assist in building an earthly temple, made with wood bricks and stones. In so doing, I neglected to take care of my physical body, which is also God's temple. I am reminded that God does not dwell in temples made with human hands (Acts 7:48). Rather, my body is God's temple (1 Corinthians 3:16–17). Therefore, I vowed to be a better steward of God's temple: my physical, mental, and spiritual being. Eugene Peterson reminds us that pastoral life can be hard on the soul. Preaching, teaching, leading, and peacemaking are but a few of the many ways we serve through the church. There can be a strain and a sure test to the failure of our inner life by preoccupation with the external.

There are advantages and disadvantages living in the rectory, adjacent to the church building. For me, residing in the rectory for twenty years was heavily demanding on my family and my personal life. This was complicated by our living in the rectory during the planning and construction phase of the building. It was like living on the job 24/7/365/20. No real day off. One can easily become toxic. Gregory the Great said, "Those who watch for the souls of those under their care must keep watch over their own souls. Inner care for the minister's soul and external care for the church are inseparable components of the pastoral craft" (*The Clergy Journal*, Vol. LXXXI, No. 8, p. 10).

Father Lionel Young III writes, "When pastors become so engrossed in the daily care of the church that they neglect the cultivation of the inward life through prayer, reading, study, and meditation, they fail the church" (*The Clergy Journal*, Vol. LXXXI, No. 8, p. 12). Once we moved out of the rectory in 2004, I was able to balance my schedule between work, leisure, prayer, reading, study, meditation, and exercise. St. Paul exhorts us to "never be lacking in zeal, but keep your spiritual fervor, serving the Lord" (Romans 12:11 NIV).

Have you ever noticed, when people host a party, they hardly eat during the festivities? They are usually so overwhelmed that they rarely sit and enjoy the party. They are taken up in making sure the guests enjoy themselves. The greater part of the first fifteen years was like hosting a party. The time I really began to smell the roses was when I sat in the congregation, which was very rare, and usually during a concert. I'm not officiating. I can just sit and savor the moment, staring at the ceiling, with its many beams, reflecting on the crane and the workmen installing the beams. Then there were times when I sat in silence, alone, in the building, meditating and acknowledging the faithfulness of God. I sure needed much more time to counteract the earlier bitterness.

Finally, in my discernment as to whether I should stay or move on, I thought of how I was transplanted to the parish, and how the right hand of God had directed my path even before I was born. It became very clear to me that the Search Committee and the vestry who elected me as the second rector were merely God's servants. The omnipotent God is the true architect of my life. Moreover, the Lord constantly reveals the purpose of my life. Hence, I prayed for divine guidance:

> Oh, God you knew me before I was born.
> You created me in my inmost parts.
> You knit me together in my mother's womb.
> You opened my lips that my mouth may show forth your praise.
> You called me like the child Samuel to serve in your Sanctuary.

You rescued me from the depth of the ocean and gave me a new lease on life.

You called me from the grafting of trees to the grafting of souls.
You were my lifeguard when I was thrown into the deep end of the pool.

You ordered my steps when I was transplanted to this parish.
You sent your guardian angel to protect me when I was in the lion's den.

You provided the lamb for the burnt offering and saved my son's life.
You have been the Chief Architect and Builder in the erection of the edifice.

Now we have dedicated this temple to your honor and glory. Notwithstanding, you do not dwell in temples made with human hands. I pause at this time to discern your will for my future ministry. My personal desire is to stay and finish the course. But whatsoever is your will, I pray that it may be done, in and through me.

Amen.

As God would have it, I remained at St. David's and assisted in putting the finishing touches to the building. This entailed burning all the mortgages; installing a new pipe organ, hardwood floors, state-of-the-art bathrooms; refurbishing the exterior walls; and initiating a multimedia ministry with live stream services.

In recognition of my ministry, someone very thoughtful gave me a book and autographed it with these words:

J. MASTINE NISBETT

Father,

By the title of this book, you are his beloved Son and he is very pleased. Congratulations!
Now go for the gold.

Love,

The Prodigal

The title of the book is *The Five-Star Church: Serving God and His People with Excellence* by Stan Toler and Alan Nelson. The book remained on the shelf in my library for a while, until one day, I picked it up, browsed through it, and readily recognized its invaluable treasure. I began reading the book and subsequently organized a two-day workshop based on it.

In short, our goal was to make the church a five-star church. Mindful of the fact that the church was more than brick, mortar, wood, and furniture, we focused on individuals and the corporate body as a whole.

We live in a culture where people go church shopping. Gone are the days when they remain a member of a congregation out of loyalty. In the book by Toler and Nelson, they quoted Tom McCaslin as saying, "People judge churches the same way they judge restaurants" (Nelson, p. 145)

In that sense, we at St. David's were determined to be a very good restaurant. We attempted to adopt the quality goals for Trinity Church as published in the book:

> We will always seek to speak an encouraging word to our guests.
> We will focus on our strengths and seek to improve our weakness.
> We will strive to build quality ministry action teams.
> We will be thoughtful and Christlike in every relationship.
> We will cultivate physical, mental, and spiritual growth.
> We will treat others as we hope others will treat us.
> We will ask, listen and hear—to determine the felt
> needs and potential of each newcomer.
> We will seek the guidance of the Holy Spirit in every decision-
> making opportunity. (Toler and Nelson, p. 76)

I do not remember which prodigal signed the book "The Prodigal." One thing I know is there have been a few prodigals. There is a temptation to rejoice when an individual leaves our congregation. Why? Is that not a contradiction? Sometimes, we preachers are good in telling people what to do. We tell them to love their enemies and to turn the other cheek. Sadly, we fail to give examples of how to love your enemies. Where possible, I tried to preach "how-to" sermons. When this is done, many congregants take notes; above all, your best sermon is your life. Lead by example, welcoming the prodigal.

The Latin word for priest is *pointex*, which means "bridge builder." Jesus Christ, our Great High Priest, is the bridge between God and ourselves. As priests, we are called to be bridge-builders, reconcilers. Isn't this what we are called to do in the sacrament of reconciliation? The parable of the prodigal son (Luke 15) is a case in point. The father never rested until his son returned home, whom he welcomed and gave a party in his honor. At St. David's, my mission has been to welcome the prodigal.

The well-known great commission of our Lord is "Go into all the world and make disciples of all nations" (Matthew 28:19). Pastors are like fishermen who let down their nets and catch various species of fish. I am a cradled Anglican Episcopalian, who is a fisher of men. I do not go seeking Anglicans or Episcopalians. Rather, I lay down the net like a fisherman and take in whatever kind of fish there is in the locality; be they Episcopalians, Anglicans, Methodists, Roman Catholics, or Baptists. We have also opened the door to Adventists and Jehovah's Witnesses.

Many years ago, a colleague of mine referred a family to my pastoral care. The husband was Episcopalian, and he insisted that his three children be nurtured in the Episcopal faith. The wife, however, was an Adventist. She faithfully dropped the children off to church, confirmation class, and the youth group. She never really participated in the church's activities; she simply brought the children out of duty. The husband, on the other hand, was not visible. One of the children had an unfortunate experience: He was knocked down by a car and remained in a coma for six months. I ministered to him and his family throughout this ordeal. With prayers, medication, and therapy, he recovered and is still with us, albeit with much physical disabilities. The parents and the physically challenged son moved to Florida. After the death of the father, the mother and son relocated to New York and reunited with the church. Today, the entire family, including the mother, worship with us. What's more, the mother has publicly expressed her faith in our midst and has received Communion in our church. Amazing. That is sowing the seed, allowing it to germinate, gently nurturing it, and allowing it to mature and bloom where it is planted.

Pastoral care could be very demanding, and even more so when there is a long pastorate. Visioneering is the periodical evaluation of the vision and realignment of the mission. Sometimes, this means dismounting the dead horse; the vision remains but the mission changes. Therefore, when a specific mission has had its run, one needs to know when to move on. This demands a creative ministry. To that end, we established an annual theme around which our activities and sermons were structured. "Empowering the Laity" and "Spiritual Tune-Up" were two of the themes we had. In empowering the laity for ministry, I divided the congregation into twelve groups to assist in the pastoral care of the parish. On the Fridays during Lent, the groups were responsible for organizing the devotion, presenting the Stations of the Cross, and providing a short meditation each week. The response was great; you got an idea where individuals were in their spiritual journey. The attendance was good. Imagine seventy people showing up for Stations of the Cross on a Friday night. In Lent of 2018, while I was on sabbatical, they did it all on their own. The coordinator for the group asked the team leaders to do research on a specific apostle for presentation during the 2019 Lenten season. In addition to all this, the group is an excellent catalyst for raising funds for the parish. One year, they raised over seventy-five thousand dollars. They bloomed where they were planted.

It's no easy task to prepare sermons as a solo priest for over three decades. Every Sunday, the faithful gathered around the table to be fed; like the wise chef who cooks the egg in different ways (scrambled, poached, fried, hard boiled, and omelet), the preacher must seek the guidance of the Holy Spirit to look at scripture with a new lens and proclaim it to contemporary society. This requires a creative ministry. In the Appendix is a Good Friday meditation given by Ms. Lorna Jones, a lay member. It was related to our theme "Spiritual Tune-Up." Her sermon was entitled "The Centurion as a Catalytic Converter." I recommend it to you. It's worth reading.

You may remember the Waco Siege, a fifty-one-day standoff between Branch Davidians and federal agents that ended on April 19, 1993, when the religious group's compound near Waco, Texas, was destroyed in a fire. This tragedy occurred during the Easter season, and it dominated the news at the time. The Gospel for the week following the fire was about the risen Christ's discourse with two disciples on the Emmaus Road (Luke 24:13–32). That Sunday, we did a dialogue sermon entitled "The Emmaus Road" in light of the Waco experience. We also dramatized the story of the blind man (John 9).

Then there was the Passion Play that I wrote, *Who's on Trial?* The play was staged for years on Palm Sunday by St. David's Drama Group, and each time, I played the part of Jesus and was crucified. There were about twenty-five people in the cast. With props, lights, and sound effects, I was told it was nothing short of an off-Broadway production. The cast members truly immersed themselves in the play and thereafter took on new names such as Judas, Pilate, and Caiaphas. Clement Thomas, an eighty-eight-year-old man, delighted himself in striking me with his cane and crowning me with the crown of thorns. The cast's self-esteem got a booster shot and latent talents were unfolded in both young and old. Randy Moses and his family were new worshipers with us. He joined the cast and was one of the soldiers. Shortly thereafter, the family officially joined the church. A year later, he was elected to the vestry. His son, Tristan, was confirmed and involved in the youth group. His daughter, Nicole, is a youth group member, attends Sunday school, is a member of the Liturgical Dance Group, and is being prepared for confirmation. The family mushroomed and bloomed where it was planted.

At the Christmas Eve service, we sang the Christmas carol, "The First Noel." As we sang the stanza:

> They looked up and saw a star
> shining in the east, beyond them far
> and to the earth it gave great light,
> And so, it continued both day and night.

J. MASTINE NISBETT

We had a star that traveled from the back of the church to the sanctuary, guided by a pulley. The star arrived at the manger scene during the singing of the fourth stanza:

> This star drew nigh to the northwest,
> o'er Bethlehem it took its rest,
> and there it did both stop and stay,
> right over the place where Jesus lay.

On December 31, 1999, the eve of the Y2K, with the anticipated problems, many feared going to Times Square to witness the annual New Year's countdown. We introduced our own New Year's ball at a watch night service and displayed it annually for the next eighteen years. The ball, of course, is not liturgical, but then what is liturgical? What is holy? What is secular? Didn't Jesus take ordinary things, like bread and wine, and make them holy? Shouldn't we too follow that example to take the ordinary things of life and give them spiritual meaning?

It should be borne in mind that this is no attempt to turn the sanctuary into a theater where people are entertained. Rather, it is designed to find new ways to proclaim the Gospel. Although God's Word does not change, it should be proclaimed with renewed freshness. We need to find new vehicles to proclaim the old, old story. If you have been blessed by God with the gift of drama, then you ought to use it to glorify God.

Of course, this all relates to culture. Each congregation has its own culture. What works at St. David's may not work at St. Mary's. The leader must know the congregation. This can be accomplished to a great extent when you have a long and meaningful relationship with a congregation.

A few years ago, we honored several organizations in our community. The goal was to deepen our relationship with our neighbors. Among those we paid homage to were teachers, law enforcement officers, elected officials, and first responders. In planning the liturgy for the Sunday when the first responders were honored, I searched for an appropriate hymn. Finding none, I was moved by the spirit to write the following hymn (it was my first piece of work in this sphere; since then I have written six others):

> "Hail to Our First Responders"
> Hail to our first responders who risk their lives for us.
> They volunteered their service in time of urgent need.
> Professionals they are not, yet readily they serve.
> Help us to follow daily their brave and noble deeds.
>
> Hail to our first responders who daily leave their homes.
> Their families may worry about their risky work.
> May God protect them daily wherever they may roam.
> Guide them and bring them safely to home, once more, again.
>
> Hail to our first responders who race to save our lives.
> They come in haste when summoned and risk their lives for us.
> Dispatched at once the call made, they readily arrive.
> In gratitude, we thank them for their unselfish love.
>
> Hail to our first responders who race to save our lives.
> They put out fires that plague us and render CPR.
> They intervene in conflicts to settle our disputes.
> How can we thank these workers for their courageous work?
>
> Hail to our first responders who bravely gave their lives.
> They risk their lives to save us and sacrifice their own.
> Grant peace to them, O Father, and comfort the bereaved.
> May we be always grateful for those who shared their lives.
> Tune: "Hail to the Lord's Anointed" (Meter 7676D)

God, our Creator, is forever creating. Jesus said, "My father has been working until now. I too am working" (John 5:17 INSV). As God's agents, we need to be open to the Holy Spirit and be creative in God's ministry.

Over the past four decades, I've had the privilege and responsibility to administer the sacrament of baptism to many individuals. However, I did not baptize any of them. While I presided at the sacrament, it is the Triune God who truly baptizes, and it is that name into which we are all baptized. This understanding was made vividly clear to me some years ago when a family, who were not members of the congregation, showed up one Sunday morning with a baby to be baptized.

I told the mother,

"I am sorry, I cannot baptize the child this morning. You did not attend the baptism class. Besides, you are not a member of this congregation. I do not mind baptizing the child, but you at least need to attend the baptism class."

"Pastor, we are sorry to have missed the class," the mother said. "We did not know it was a requirement, but seeing that we are here, can you grant us the favor of baptizing the child?"

"I am afraid not."

"Why?"

"As a pastor, my role is to preserve the teachings of the church."

"I truly understand that, but does that prevent you from baptizing this little baby?"

"With no disrespect to you, Jesus once said, 'It is not right to take the children's bread and cast it to the dogs.'" She looked intently at me. I could see the anger boiling up in her. "Do not misunderstand me. I am not calling you a dog. What Jesus was saying, and what I am saying, is we are accountable for our actions."

"Yeah, but Jesus also said, 'Suffer the little children to come unto me and forbid them not.'"

I was stunned. I paused and then said, "Okay, I'll baptize the child with the understanding that you attend a special baptism class on Wednesday at 6 p.m."

"Thank you so much for your consideration. We will attend the class."

Jodie, the baby, was baptized, grew up in the church, became an acolyte, and participated in the church's activities. She is now an engineer working for Boeing in California. On the twenty-seventh anniversary of her baptism, she flew from Los Angeles to deliver a very inspiring message at the Sunday Eucharist. Although she resides out of state, she continues to support the church financially, and over the years, she has showered me with many gifts. Today, her family continues to be very active members of St. David's. An incredible story.

Bloom Wherever God Plants You

God does not need any apologists. God is the one who does the baptism. We are only the agents. Jodie and her family are among the many I was privileged to nurture and enable to bloom where they were planted.

As a nurturer, one must look out for young, tender plants. One hymn writer puts it:

"Loving Shepherd of thy sheep keep thy lamb in safety keep; nothing can thy power withstand, none can pluck me from thy hand."

Effective ministry means to accept people where they are and help them to bloom into faithful children of God. At St. David's, we keep the children involved with many activities, such as the Steel Orchestra Ministry, Liturgical Dance Group, Youth Group, Junior Choir, Acolyte Ministry, and Sunday school. So it was not unusual at the Family Service, on the third Sunday of the month, to have the children switching roles. They serve at the altar, sing in the choir, participate in the liturgical dance, and play in the Steel Orchestra. These young people dedicate their weekends in preparing themselves for their ministry at St. David's.

Our Steel Orchestra, "Praises in Steel," as it is called, has blossomed tremendously. It has done concerts in neighborhood churches and beyond, performing at City Hall, our diocesan convention, weddings, and more.

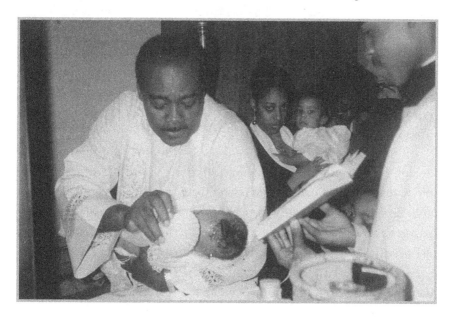

Father Nisbett officiating at Jodie's baptism.

Our liturgical dancers have outdone themselves, as they participated at luncheons, at concerts, and at a Easter Sunday sunrise service at Jones Beach. One of the dancers, Alleyne Grant, is aspiring to become a member of the Alvin Ailey American Dance Theater. Another of our young ladies, Shannon Whittaker, is majoring in African studies at Stony Brook University. She continues to pursue her passion for music by participating in the choir while holding a position on the Executive Board for the university's Gospel Choir. Chad Maccou is a rising self-taught musician; Andrew Yarde and Reniece McIntyre play piano and organ. Many of these youngsters were baptized at St. David's. It is a joy to see them grow and blossom.

Many years ago, I held a little baby, Aaliyah Fernandez, in my arms when she was baptized. I saw her grow to become an articulate young lady. She was nurtured in the Sunday school, Youth Group, Acolyte Ministry, Liturgical Dance Group, Youth Choir, Drama Group, and Steel Orchestra Ministry. Additionally, she was a youth delegate for the diocesan convention, and in 2014, she was one of fifteen youth from the Diocese of Long Island who attended the Episcopal Youth Event at Villanova University. There were over twelve hundred other youth from eighty dioceses around the world. The preachers at the event were the former Presiding Bishop, Katharine Jefferts Schori, the current Presiding Bishop, Michael Curry, and several others. Aaliyah is graduated in May 2019 with a bachelor of arts in psychology and a bachelor of science in human development. She continues to serve at the altar and was the typist who typed this chapter of the manuscript. This is another one of our success stories. Children blooming where they are planted.

Just as how I do not baptize anyone, so too, I do not marry anyone except Enid, my wife. Yes, in my forty-four years as a priest, I have officiated at many wedding ceremonies. I am still in touch with Benjamin and Ernestine Jerrod, the first couple whose wedding ceremony I was happy to conduct. I am even more ecstatic to have officiated at Toussaint & Maudlyn James' wedding ceremony over forty years ago. I subsequently presided at their children's and grandchildren's baptism, solemnized their daughter's wedding, and, sadly, conducted the funeral service of their grandchild. One of the joys of pastoral longevity is to be able to nurture three generations in the same family.

My ministry to the Manahan family is even more interesting. Note the following:

In August 1985, I officiated at the twenty-fifth wedding anniversary of Dorrell and Norma Manahan. This was my first matrimonial service at St. David's.

In September 1990, I officiated at the wedding ceremony of the Manahans' daughter, Paula.

On December 6, 1992, I officiated at the baptism of the Manahans' grandson, Kevin. Later that same day, I conducted the funeral service for Dorrell Manahan. It was the third baptism and the first funeral in the new edifice.

In July 1996, I officiated at the baptism of the Manahans' grandson, Kyle.

On April 13, 2019, I conducted the memorial service for Norma Manahan. It was my last funeral and memorial service as rector of the parish.

Baptism marks our adoption into God's family. On the other hand, death is our transition from our mortal life to a life of immortality with our Creator. Ministering to these two vital areas of one's life in one day is indeed remarkable. But ministering them to the same family, on the same day, is even more amazing and rewarding. It should be noted that the Manahans were not always visible in the life of St. David's. But this is precisely how the will of God is often revealed: in the very people we least expect. In the story of the incarnation, God chose a peasant teenager to be the mother of our Lord. The baby Jesus was born in a stable in a manger, not in the king's palace. Ultimately, God's redemptive work was completed on a cross; the place you'd least expect it. This is very much like the crack in the pavement where a plant blooms, despite its limited resources. Ministry does not get better than that.

At our acolytes reunion, seventeen young men and women joined a long procession into the sanctuary. There were robed in black cassocks and white surplices. They once served at God's altar. They laundered their robes and returned to the sanctuary to worship God. What a glorious reunion that was. Even more so, I heard their stories as they reflected on their past and learned that I had some influence in the shaping of their lives. How gratifying that was. I hope I had the same impact on the other acolytes who were not able to attend the service. Are they all blooming in God's garden, wheresoever that may be?

Also present at the reunion service was a young man I held as a baby when he was baptized. Seated beside him was a young lady who was also nurtured at St. David's, which is their garden of Eden. The two seem to be growing in their relationship, blooming where they were planted. The reunion of these acolytes was part of the nurturing of the plant, the nurturing of their faith.

The collect for that day was:

> Stir up thy power, O Lord, and with great might come among us; and, because we are sorely hindered by our sins, let thy bountiful grace and mercy speedily help and deliver us; through Jesus Christ our Lord, to whom, with thee and the Holy Ghost, be honor and glory, world without end. Amen. (Third Sunday of Advent, p. 160 BCP)

It was Stir-Up Sunday. Stirring up the soil around the plant, which is vital in the plant's life. Interestingly, the Old Testament lesson for the previous Sunday read thus:

> Take off the garment of your sorrow and affliction, O Jerusalem, and put on forever the beauty of the glory from God. Put on the robe of the righteousness that comes from God; put on your head the diadem of the glory of the Everlasting; for God will show your splendor everywhere under heaven. For God will give you evermore the name, "Righteous Peace, Godly Glory." Arise, O Jerusalem, stand upon the height; look toward the east, and see your children gathered from west and east at the word of the Holy One, rejoicing that God has remembered them. For they went out from you on foot, led away by their enemies; but God will bring them back to you, carried in glory, as on a royal throne. For God has ordered that every high mountain and the everlasting hills be made low and the valleys filled up, to make level ground, so that Israel may walk safely in the glory of God. The woods and every fragrant tree have shaded Israel at God's command. For God will lead Israel with joy, in the light of his glory, with the mercy and righteousness that come from him. (Baruch 5:1–9 NRSV)

Who knows? Perhaps, just perhaps, those acolytes adorning themselves in their washed robes were spiritually putting on their garment of salvation. Maybe this was precisely what they needed in their spiritual journey: the stirring up of their spiritual life. The reunion of the acolytes took me back to my early childhood when I, too, served at God's altar. The following Sunday, one of the acolytes, Miguel Clark, returned with his wife, Alissa (I had solemnized their marriage and officiated at their children's baptism). Of course, the joy of longevity is to witness all this in your ministry.

Throughout my ministry, I have tried to foster vocations to the ordained ministry. Today, I rejoice that at least five people who had been under my tutelage have responded to God's call to the ordained ministry. The Reverends Maxine Barnett, Selina Joseph, and Alister Rawlins are priests in the Anglican Episcopal Church. Loretta Ramsey was a teenager at St. George's Anglican, Antigua when I ministered there. Currently, she is a bishop in Pennsylvania and does missionary work. Some years ago, I attended a funeral service at a Methodist church in the Bronx. The pastor, the Rev. Dr. Gordon Edwards, immediately recognized me and introduced me to the congregation as his former teacher. Dr. Edwards is not only a pastor; he is also a practicing psychotherapist.

Michael Wilkinson was nurtured at St. David's and is involved in Christ Ministry in the Carolinas.

They all bloom where they are planted. When they bloom, I bloom, the church blooms, and more importantly, God is glorified.

The nurturing of the Reverend Maxine Barnett is of particularly interesting. She was a founding member of the Young Adult Group, which was organized on May 11, 1991. It was the very day we began excavating the site for the new building. She was a Sunday school teacher, superintendent of the Sunday school, vestry member, and Eucharistic minister. Led by the spirit, I thought she was a suitable candidate for the ordained ministry. I gave her some literature to read during a period of convalescence. Thereafter, I periodically gave her a little nudge.

Then one day, she said to me, "Father, I think I am ready."

Catching me off guard, I responded, "Ready for what?"

"To test my vocation."

That is the beauty of nurturing. You sow the seed. You water it. You stir up the soil around it and allow the Holy Spirit to do the rest.

Responding to God's call is not limited to the ordained ministry. The followers of John the Baptist asked what they should do in preparing for the coming Messiah. John did not ask them to join the church. He simply told them to exercise whatever ministry they were already engaged in (Luke 3:7–18). In other words, bloom where you are planted.

Not long ago, I was on a cruise with friends and several parishioners from St. David's. One lady, who is a frequent cruiser with us, said to me,

"Father Nisbett, I must tell you, on our last cruise, you said in your sermon that it is possible that someone may be going through a rough time in his or her marriage. This vacation could be a time for reflection and relaxation as you discern the future of your relationship. When I heard you said that, I was in awe because you did not know my circumstances. I felt it was God speaking to me through you."

"Oh, really!"

"Yes, Father, I could not believe what I was hearing."

"And what was the outcome?"

"I must tell you: You saved my marriage. I was going to leave my husband, but I used that vacation to reconsider my decision, and for that, I am eternally grateful to you and God because you were God's messenger that day."

She is just one of the many people who have made similar remarks.

In March 2018, I visited my home parish in Nevis. There, I met a young man, Stedroy Williams, whom I taught in Sunday school. He said to me, "Do you remember *Saul of Tarsus*?"

I was not sure what he meant and said, "No, I do not recall."

"You do not remember the play you directed?"

"Oh, yes, I do recall."

"Well, I want to tell you, that play made a lasting impression on me."

Many times, when I walk the streets of St. John's, Antigua, or am on a street in New York City, I am suddenly embraced by someone who greets me.

"Hi, Mr. Nisbett. So good to see you."

I am often at a loss and say, "Please remind me who you are."

"You do not remember me? You were my history teacher at All Saints Secondary School."

Some reach for their pocketbook or wallet, show me a picture of their family, and proceed to tell me their life story. You realize that you have made an impact on their lives. One of these former students became my electrician. Many of them are blooming in their various spheres of life, and I am happy that I helped nurture them.

One of the greatest compliments I've ever received is to have someone name their child after me. This has happened not once, not twice, but three times. When I sojourned in Antigua, a mother who was not a member of my parish, but an Anglican nonetheless, named her son Mastine. What motivated her to do this, I am not sure. It could have been the uniqueness of the name, or she may have seen me as a good role model for her son. I hope she was not disappointed.

At St. David's, there was a young lady who grew up in the church and subsequently went off to college to further her education. She returned later and asked me to officiate at her wedding ceremony. When she had problems conceiving, I prayed with the couple and blessed them. Shortly thereafter, she conceived, and they named the child Joshua after me.

Then there was another young lady who was nurtured at St. David's. She was very anxious about having a child. I referred her to the story of Hannah in the Bible. Hannah, you will recall, was childless and prayed desperately for a son. She pledged she would dedicate him to God's service. Her prayers were answered, and she subsequently dedicated her son, Samuel, to God's service. About six months after I counseled the young lady, she conceived. Several months later, I officiated at the baptism of her son, Samuel.

These families, advertently or inadvertently, grafted me into their family tree, where I probably will remain for generations to come. What an honor. I will bloom where I least expected.

William Durham was the first African American who was brave enough to purchase a house in Cambria Heights, New York. Durham encountered much turmoil for his courageous act. He and his family received death threats. His house was vandalized, and a cross was burned on his lawn. Through it all, he remained steadfast and eventually gained the respect of his neighbors. Subsequently, he earned the title "Mayor of Cambria Heights." Durham was a pioneer for blacks in the neighborhood. He was a disciple of the late Dr. Martin Luther King Jr., who advocated peaceful reconciliation through nonviolence. This incredible story was never published until 2004, when I met this quiet, unassuming, nonviolent champion of peace and reconciliation in my research on the community. With some effort, Durham's story as an unsung hero was lifted up. He was recognized at St. David's on February 23, 2003, as part of our Black History program. Subsequently, he received an award at City Hall, and the street where he once lived will be renamed in his honor. He bloomed where he was planted. He was like a crack in the sidewalk with no soil, but that crevice became his oasis where he and others bloomed.

Ironically, in 1961, when Durham did his pioneering heroic service in the community, I was still attending school in my home country. On Sunday, February 2, 1985, the Presentation of the Lord in the Temple, and my farewell service from my former parish St. George's, Antigua, one of the lectionary readings for that day was the Song of Simeon:

> Lord, now lettest thou thy servant depart in peace,
> according to thy word;
> for mine eyes have seen thy salvation,
> which thou hast prepared before the face of all people,
> to be a light to lighten the Gentiles,
> and to be the glory of thy people Israel (Nunc
> dimittis, Luke 2:29–32, p. 66 BCP).

A light to lighten the Gentiles.

I relate to this event for the following reason: I think that in some ways, the Durham family was like the Gentiles, while the original Caucasians were like the Jews. My going forth from St. George's to the now black congregation in Cambria Heights felt like the fulfillment of Simeon's prophecy. God showed the light before the face of all the people of Cambria Heights.

I've often been at the bedside of loved ones who were about to make a transition from this world. Sometimes, it involves giving them permission to make the transition, so they can continue to bloom in the hereafter. On July 2, 2009, I sat at the bedside of Estelle Holden (a centenarian) in Franklin General Hospital and witnessed her breathing her last breath. Then there was Michelle Austin's mother at Brookville Hospital in

Brooklyn. One Sunday morning, Michelle requested the last rites for her mother. Immediately after my last service, I rushed to the hospital. The faithful soul was still alive. She was conscious, but soon after I gave her Holy Communion and anointed her in the sacrament of Holy Unction, she expired.

The Reverend James Manning was a former colleague, and I had the privilege of ministering to him in his final days. When I arrived at the hospital, some parishioners told me that he was not responding. When I called him by his name, he opened his eyes and participated in the prayers. I anointed him, and shortly thereafter, he passed away. Having been planted and rooted in the Christian faith, he made his transition; I hope he will continue to bloom in his new garden.

"Bloom Where You Are Planted" means not just to provide shade and fruits for the immediate surroundings. The prophet Isaiah exhorted his people to spread out and think big:

"Clear lots of ground for your tents! Make your tents large. Spread out! Think big. Use plenty of rope. Drive the tent peg deep. You are going to need lots of elbow room for your growing family" (Isaiah 54:2–3 the Message).

Cognizant of the prophet's exhortation, we extended our mission to include St. John's Hospital Auxiliary Ministry in Far Rockaway and Berega Orphanage in Tanzania. We provide financial assistance to the orphanage. With our assistance, they completed a new recreation room. Sewing machines were provided to assist in teaching the ladies how to sew and make school uniforms for the children. In January 2018, Enid and I visited the orphanage and confirmed that there was a genuine need there.

In the early church, Jesus told his disciples they would be witnesses of him, beginning in Jerusalem and going throughout the earth. In like manner, our witnessing began in Cambria Heights and has reached many parts of the earth, including Tanzania. Thanks to Mother Maxine Barnett, whose response to God's call initiated our relationship with Berega. Then, of course, there are Leslie and Carol Faulkner, who have been our liaisons with Berega. Blooming where you are planted, therefore, is not confined to any specific locality. We are expected to bloom wherever we are and wherever God's people are (that is, the whole world).

Regionally, we donated funds to the city of New Orleans following Hurricane Katrina. After hurricanes Irma and Maria, we donated twelve thousand dollars to the Diocese of North East Caribbean and Aruba. We participated with "Food for the Poor" in building a house in Jamaica, West Indies. We also provided funds for the Children's Hospital in Jerusalem. These were some of the outreach ministries, blooming where God planted us.

Father Nisbett and Mrs. Nisbett speaking with Bishop Sehaba at the Anglican Catherdral in Morogoro Tanzania

Completion of the recreation room at the Berega Orphanage with assistance from St. David's Church.

Sewing machines at the Berega Orphanage provided by the Episcopal Church Women.

CHAPTER 9

REACH AND TOUCH

As stated earlier, this narrative journey began with the suggestions of the Rev. Canon Cecily Broderick, Dr. Betty Carrington, and Euclid Jordan, who urged me to write about my long tenure at St. David's. What a rewarding spiritual experience it has been. The exercise has helped me to reflect on life's experiences and recognize God's presence throughout the journey, especially in those times when the presence seemed obscured. I am more convinced that the promptings did not originate with the three individuals. Rather, God was the origin.

The setting for the first chapter of the narrative, you will recall, was Nevis, the land of my birth. In writing this last chapter, it became apparent that the journey did not originate in Nevis but in Ghana, the homeland of my ancestors. This revelation occurred while on a pilgrimage to Africa.

On Sunday January 28, 2018, Enid and I had the privilege of worshiping at St. Cyprian's Anglican Cathedral in Kumasi, Ghana. The Rev. Canon Frederick Opare-Addo had previously introduced us to the dean of the cathedral, the Very Rev. Elvis Achampong, who was very gracious to us. On hearing that we were West Indians and probably from the Asante tribe, he said, "Welcome, my brother and sister. Welcome to our cathedral."

Bloom Wherever God Plants You

Dean Nisbett participating in the liturgy at St. Cyprian's Anglican Cathedral in Kumasi Ghana

I was given a prominent seat in the sanctuary, while Enid sat near the altar. The service commenced with the choir processing around the interior of the cathedral, chanting Psalm 122: "I was glad when they said unto me, let us go into the House of the Lord." I thought this was most appropriate for our visit. The hymnbook used was *The Ancient and Modern Hymnbook*, one I was familiar with from early childhood. Likewise, the musical arrangement for the Gloria in Excelsis Deo and the Nicene Creed was Merbecke, an equally familiar one.

There were several acolytes in attendance, robed in red cassocks and white surplices. Among them was a little boy carrying the boat with the incense. As I looked at him, I remembered my childhood days when I too was a boat-boy. The dean had me fully involved in the liturgy, singing the Gospel, administering Holy Communion, and blessing individuals, notwithstanding the fact that I was not robed, just dressed in a clergy shirt. I resonated fully with the service. It was like worshiping with my home congregation. I felt the presence of my ancestors, particularly my deceased parents. At one time, I even felt a little emotionally choked up. I had a euphoric feeling when I left the cathedral, an elation that remained with me for the rest of the day.

Reflecting on the day's events, I thought of this manuscript. It was gratifying yet humbling to think that we, the children of the African Diaspora, could join our sisters and brothers in such an inspiring liturgy.

One of the sites where the slaves had their last bath in Ghana

Sadly, though, the spiritual euphoria was short-lived. The next day, we toured a slave market and two large castles, where the slaves sat in dungeons, awaiting their shipment to the Americas and the Caribbean. The emotions I experienced within the next two days were alarming. It was like being on a comfortable flight when suddenly, the airplane takes a nosedive that jolts every nerve of yours, and you wonder whether you are still airborne.

As a student of history, I was not completely naïve to the plight of the slaves. However, reading about it is not enough. But visiting those sacred grounds, sacred because human blood was spilt there, was like reliving the traumatic experience of my ancestors.

Our guided tour took us to an ancient slave market in Assin Manso. This was the place where the captured and shackled slaves were gathered and later auctioned, but not before they took their last bath in their home country. The shackled slaves were assembled near a river but were not allowed to bathe in the flowing river, for fear they may escape. Instead, they were bathed in the nearby stagnant water. Being shackled, they could not bathe themselves. Consequently, the trunk of a bamboo tree was used to pour water over the slaves. Later, their skin was oiled to make them look presentable for the auction.

Following the bath, the slaves traveled through the bushes to the auction site. As they journeyed through the bushes, they planted pineapples trees. This was one way of establishing a trail to the market. In other words, the shackled slaves were still working on their way to the market.

After the auction the slaves were branded with identification marks. They were then huddled like animals and taken to the coast, some thirty miles away, to be stored in a dungeon and await shipment to the Caribbean and the Americas. The slaves' journey to the coast reminded me of our Lord's walk to Golgotha. Perhaps in some ways, it was more physically exhausting than that of our Lord's. Remember, they were shackled, and the journey was about thirty miles. No, unlike Jesus, they did not have Simon of Cyrene to assist them. And yes, some died on the way.

The dungeon at Cape Coast Castle

On arrival at the castle, the slaves were placed in dark dungeons with very little light or ventilation. Some of them lose their sight when reintroduced to sunlight. Packed like sardines, there were about three hundred male slaves in a thirty-foot room with no bathroom. They defecated, urinated, vomited, ate, and slept in the same area. The rebellious ones were chained; locked away in a dark cell; deprived of food, water, light, and oxygen; and left to die. Their bodies were dumped into the nearby Atlantic Ocean. This was to serve as a deterrent for the other slaves.

The door connecting the dungeon to the Door of no Return

The female slaves were often raped by their captors. On arrival at the castle, they were examined. The chosen ones were escorted to the governor's quarters for his sexual pleasure. Unyielding slaves were punished. Pregnant slaves were spared the Atlantic voyage ordeal and taken elsewhere to give birth to their offspring. These mulattoes were educated and given supervisory jobs at the castle, thus creating a class system.

We should note the slaves could be held in the dungeon up to ten weeks, awaiting a ship's arrival. Then the next phase of their journey commenced, as the shackled slaves entered a narrow passage to the Door of No Return, en route to the Americas or the Caribbean. No kiss, no hug, no goodbye. Off to an unknown destination. The unwilling immigrant. No wonder some committed suicide, jumping overboard or starving themselves to death rather than subjecting themselves to their masters.

The damage done to West Africa was irreversible and immeasurable. Over six million slaves were exported as cargo, unwilling immigrants to the Americas, the Caribbean, and elsewhere. Historians believed that between 10 and 15 percent of those people perished at sea, never reaching their destination.

Door of No Return

We should never overlook the role the African chiefs played in the slave business. They were just as guilty for selling their fellow Africans into slavery. To that end, a body comprising all the country's traditional kings and chiefs placed a plaque on both the Elmina and Cape Coast Castle, asking for forgiveness. This body is known as the Ghana House of Chiefs. The plaque states their anguish over their ancestors, expresses hospitality to those who may return, and vowed never again to do such injustice to humanity.

The part that really got to me was to discover that the Anglican Church had a chapel over the male dungeon at the Cape Coast Castle. I knew that the church was intricately involved with slavery, but I must confess, I did not know the true depth of their involvement. The United Society for the Propagation of the Gospel (USPG), an evangelical arm of the Anglican Church, was heavily involved in slavery. At the Elmina Castle, the Roman Catholic Church had their chapel over the female dungeon.

Akosua Adoma Perbi stated, "Traditional religion in Ghana was based on the belief in a Supreme God, the Creator. The Akan called him 'Nyame,' the Ga Nyonmo; the Eve and Adangene Mawu, the Gonja Epoore; the Manprusi Nwuni and the Nayiuum. This God was so great and so far off that He needed to be worshiped through intermediaries—the lesser gods and the ancestors. The gods were deemed to inhabit rivers, trees, mountains, etc." (*A History of Indigenous Slavery in Ghana*, pp. 101–102). This practice was certainly not unique to Ghana. The Egyptians worshiped the golden calf, and Apostle Paul found a temple in Athens with an inscription "To the Unknown God" (Acts 17:33). Paul, with much care, informed his audience who the Unknown God is, that is, the God who created heaven and the earth and all that is therein.

The door connecting the dungeon to the Door of no Return It was pointed out by our tour guide that prior to the arrival of the Europeans, there was a Tabiri Shrine on the very site of the male dungeon at the Cape Coast Castle. This was a sacred worship place for the Africans. In 1565, the Portuguese built a travel lodge on the site and named it Cabo Corso. In 1653, the Swedes expanded on it, made a permanent fort, and called it Carolusberg. Finally, the British captured it in 1655 and extended it to a big castle. The African sacred place of worship was captured and changed ownership by three European countries, who often came under the disguise of religion. That sacred place of worship was desecrated, turned into a dungeon, and became the death bed of the Africans. The Tabiri Shrine was captured and returned to the site many years later.

If the Africans were pagans, as many Europeans thought, then how do we describe the Europeans? Capturing and desecrating a place of worship is bad enough. But turning the place into a dungeon, to store human beings in an inhumane manner that often led to their death, is nothing short of sacrilegious. Worst of all, doing it in the name of God is deplorable. Words cannot explain the depth of my feeling when I learned of the plight and sufferings of my ancestors. The floodgates flung wide open as tears watered my eyes. This experience reminded me of Jesus weeping over the city of Jerusalem (Luke 19:41–44).

On arrival at Cape Coast Castle, the slaves were taken to the chapel, where they were baptized and given English names. They were then dispersed to their plight in the dungeon. There is some ambivalence over the baptizing of the Africans. If they were not human beings and had no soul, which would therefore make them beyond redemption, then why baptize them? On the other hand, if they are human beings and therefore eligible for baptism, then the baptism makes them equal to their master. They become brothers and sisters in Christ. This should be reflected in their relationship with each other. How then can anyone justify enslaving, dehumanizing, and destroying fellow Christians? Was the baptism a hoax?

The Gospel tells us that Jesus went into the wilderness immediately after his baptism. There, he was tested by the devil. Ironically, the slaves were taken to the dungeon immediately after their baptism. There, they too were tested by the devil, tested even to the point of death. Was the purpose of their baptism to lead them into a gruesome death?

In the wilderness, Jesus fasted forty days and forty nights. That was a choice he made. In his hunger, he was tempted to turn stones into bread. The slaves did not have a choice. They were fed twice per day with food thrown into the dungeon from a trap door. This was not manna from above. Most likely, some were not fed. It was the survival of the fittest, and some preferred to starve themselves to death.

There was as sharp contrast between the dungeon and the castle above. The chambers of the castle were extravagant, devoid of stench and filth, unlike the dungeon below. The governor's and officers' quarters were spacious, with beautiful parquet floors and scenic views of the blue Atlantic Ocean. And of course, there was the chapel, where the governor and officers worshipped on Sundays and then went about their daily activities, completely detached from the unfathomable human misery and suffering they had consciously inflicted.

Witnessing the great disparity between the castle and the dungeon, I recalled the prophet Amos's words: "Alas for those who lie on beds of ivory, and lounge on their couches, and eat lambs from the flock, and calves from the stall; who sing idol songs to the sound of harp, … Who drink wine from bowls, anoint themselves with the finest oils, but are not grieved over the ruin of Joseph" (Amos 6:4–6).

I also remembered a stanza from the old hymn, "All Things Bright and Beautiful, All Creatures Great and Small":

> The rich man in his castle,
> the poor man at his gate.
> God made them high and lowly
> and ordered their estate.

That stanza has now been removed, but this was the thinking of the day. Deleting the stanza could be merely academic. Sadly, that philosophy is still practiced in our community, in the world, and even within the church.

My spirit was broken when I learned the depth of the sufferings of our ancestors. What disturbed me so much was the fact that I am associated with the very church that practiced this grave inhumanity. The euphoria that I left with after the liturgy at St. Cyprian's Cathedral had completely dissipated. I was not the only one who had this anguished feeling. There was an Englishwoman who accompanied us on a similar tour to the Elmina Castle. She said as a British citizen, she was embarrassed by her church's involvement in such devious practices.

Enid tried to console her, saying, "We cannot do anything about the past, but we can, and should, make a difference now and for the future."

This she readily agreed to.

The Rev. Margaret J. Marcuson, in her book, *Leaders Who Last*, said, "The past does not determine the future, but it has an influence. We do not stop with the past, of course, or even the present. The past is a prelude to the future. Clear thinking in the present and vision for the future are critically important to lasting leadership" (Marcuson, p. 31).

The day after our visit to the castle, I tried to reconcile the Sunday's worship experience with that of the castle's. For me, the problem was, "How do I bloom where I am planted?" As a cradled Anglican, one who is always proud and ready to defend the faith, the question was, "How can I bloom in a church whose hands are bloodied by injustice and greed?" I felt ashamed to be associated with such an oppressive church that dehumanized my ancestors. I pondered over this manuscript. I wrestled like Jacob with God, asking how he could plant me in such an oppressive church and expect me to bloom?

I thought of my ancestors. I thought of those who perished at the hands of their masters. I thought of the survivors, the unsung heroes, including those who survived the brutal capture, those who survived that terrifying journey from the villages to the coast, who survived the ordeal of the dungeon, going to hell and returning, who survived that deadly transatlantic voyage, who survived the destruction of their family life, who survived the servitude of the plantation system, who continue to survive slavery of any kind.

As I thought about my ancestors, I remembered my parents. They were nurtured in the Anglican church, despite her flaws. They introduced me to the said church. This was where I was nurtured and nurtured others.

My contemplation took me to a crossroad. I could have easily grown disillusioned and become an agnostic. I could have easily said that Christianity is a "white man's religion," as some have argued. But I remembered the God who carried me throughout my life, the God who transcends religion, the God who remains faithful even when we are not, the God who loves us, despite our shortcomings.

After much thought, I remembered the story of Joseph in the Old Testament. His brothers had sold him into slavery. By divine providence, Joseph's life was saved, and he became the governor of Egypt during a great famine. When the governor revealed himself to his siblings, who had journeyed to Egypt to buy food, he told them, "Do not be distressed or angry with yourselves because you have sold me here. God sent me before you to preserve life.... So it was not you who sent me here, but God" (Genesis 45:5–8).

Meditating on the text, I was led to believe that all that God had done in and through me was to empower me to help change the narrative. It was an epiphany moment. Oh, my God, is that the reason you called me into the ministry?

Our God is an awesome God. First, God calls you. God enables you to do God's will, and then you are informed why. My hope is that I have been faithful to the Lord's cause. As I reflected on the great task of purifying the church, the words of the prophet Isaiah came to mind:

No matter how long or loud or often you pray,
I'll not be listening. And do you know why?
Because you've been tearing people to pieces, and your hands are bloody.
Go home and wash up. Clean up your act. (Isaiah 1:14 the Message)

I then prayed the following prayer:
"Gracious Father, we pray for thy holy Catholic Church. Fill it with all truth, in all truth, with all peace. Where it is corrupt, purify it; where it is in error, direct it; where in any thing is amiss, reform it. Where it is right, strengthen it; where it is in want, provide for it; where it is divided, reunite it; for the sake of Jesus Christ, thy Son, our Savior. Amen" (BCP 816).

Isaiah's message was certainly relevant during the period of the transatlantic slave trade. The thing that struck me most at Cape Coast Castle and Elmina was the story of the Reverend Phillip Quarque, who was born in 1741 in Ghana. He migrated to London at an early age, with the assistance of the USPG. There, he was educated and ordained a priest in the Anglican Church. He became the first Anglican priest from Ghana. Subsequently, Reverend Quarque returned to Ghana with his English wife to be the chaplain at Cape Coast. Sadly, however, his ministry was limited to the education of the mulattoes. He was prohibited by the USPG from ministering to his fellow Ghanaians who were in the dungeon. He became a part of the oppressive system. He chose not to rock the boat; while he ministered to the mulattoes and worshiped in the chapel, his African brothers remained in the dungeon below. He did not have the courage of Moses, who lived in Pharaoh's house but led a revolt against the injustice done to his brothers. Perhaps, just perhaps, his African brothers heard the singing coming from the chapel above. The Africans could not raise their hands in praise because they were shackled. However, they were probably moved by the music; they may have raised their hearts and minds, but no one touched them, and so they remained in their plight.

I had a quick flashback of my religious experience at St. Cyprian's Cathedral a few days earlier. I wondered whether Reverend Quarque's experience was like mine. Did religion, which came wrapped in colonialism, mesmerize him rather liberate him?

Father Quarque was the first Ghanaian priest. Centuries later, I too was ordained a priest and became one of the first indigenous priests in the postcolonial era. Quarque's ministry led me to reflect on my own ministry. I visited Cape Coast Castle on the eve of my retirement, after forty-three years in the ordained ministry. Quarque's story left an indelible question in my mind: was I part of the status quo or part of the liberation movement?

I was convinced that I was called to help change the narrative. Of course, doing this single handedly would be impossible, but a year and half later I was asked to conduct a retreat for the seminarians at Codrington College Barbados. This was an ideal place to begin. If there is going to be a change in the narrative the future leaders of the church would have to be involved. In retrospect, I believe that it was part of God's providential plan that I should take the message to the seminarians. This reminds me of the Apostle Paul insisting on having his case heard in Rome. (Acts 26: 26 -32) Rome at that time was the capital of the world. If he could only get his message to Rome then in all probability it would be dispersed to all parts of the world.

However, when I agreed to conduct the retreat the "changing of the narrative" was furthest from my mind. I went to the college with no such agenda. In fact, the theme of the retreat was based on the book "Listening Hearts. Discerning call in Community."

The epiphany came on my first evening at the college. Sitting on the back porch of the principal's residence on a cloudless moonlight night. Dr Michael Clarke, the principal and I enjoying the wonders of God's creation. He pointed out the vastness of Codrington Estate. Looking straight ahead was a large area of unoccupied land that bordered the ocean.

Codrington College Barbados   *Entrance to Codrington College*

Dean Nisbett, Dr. Clarke, and seminarians at Codrington College

A view of the Atlantic Ocean from the principal's residence

"What ocean is that?" I asked.

"The Atlantic Ocean." Dr Clarke replied.

"And what lies beyond the horizon?"

"Ghana." he said.

"Really!" I was somewhat intrigued by the answer but I said nothing further on the topic.

After our social interaction I returned to my room and immediately proceeded the quest to locate the two countries on the world's map. Thanks to google.

"Aha!" their latitude is comparable. Moreover, Barbados is the most eastern of all the Caribbean Islands. Strategically located, this confirms why Barbados was the first stop for the slave ships after the transatlantic voyage.

The next day I sat on the back porch once again gazing at the Atlantic Ocean. I recalled the Cape Coast Castle in Ghana. I visualized the slaves going through the "door of no return" and placed like cargo on ships to begin the long perilous journey across the Atlantic. I imagined their wailing as they were forced to leave their families, friends, and their home country.

I looked at the ocean, the silent witness and said:

Oh sea, what did you see?

You are the exclusive witness. Tell me, what exactly did you see?

Did you see torrential storms?

How high were the waves?

Tell me about the ships that crossed your ocean.

Tell me oh sea. What did you see?

Did you see dead bodies thrown overboard?

Did you see living human beings thrown overboard to lighten the ship's cargo in times of emergency?

Did you see others desperately jumping overboard taking their own lives?

Were they devoured by sharks?

Were the ships raided of their precious cargo, by the pirates of the sea?

Tell me, oh sea, you, silent witness what did you see?

How many dead bodies were buried on your ocean bed?

Was it a dozen? A hundred?

A thousand? Or thousands?
Or were there millions? Or did you lose track of counting?
Tell me great sea, you, silent witness what precisely did you see?
Tell me, is their any other ocean that has a burial place larger than yours
Tell me great sea, you, silent witness what did you see?

As I contemplated, I imagined the ships approaching the port in Barbados. The merchants and planters looking eagerly at the ships as they advanced to the shore. They gathered at the dock like the villagers gathered around the fishermen to find out the catch of the day. But there was a difference here. The villagers were looking for fish, while the merchants and planters were looking for slaves for their estates.

The ships docked and the slaves who were submerged in the hole of the ship breathed a sigh of relief as they inhaled a breath of fresh air. They were almost crippled after being stocked like sardines for the long duration of the voyage. They were malnourished. Their vision was impaired with the sudden blast of sunlight as they emerged from the hole of the ship. Emotionally, they were drained having being severed from their families, friends, and country. They agonized over the gruesome death of their colleagues. Depressed they certainly were, but spiritually they survived.

Upon arrival they were hurriedly washed, oiled, and were expected to put on their best appearance for the auction sale. There they were manhandled like commodities on the shelves in the supermarket. When it was all finished, they went their separate ways to different plantations. Sadly, another wedge was driven into the family structure.

Did we ever stop to acknowledge the strength of these men and women? They survived the brutal capture. They survived the long dangerous journey from the villages to the coast notwithstanding they were shackled. They survived the ordeal of the dungeon. They survived that long treacherous journey across the Atlantic, many times being sea sick. Now their fate will be determined on the plantation.

It was with this agonizing background that I entered the chapel at Codrington College the next morning for meditation at 6 am, morning prayer at 6 30 am, and the Eucharist at 7 am. I found it difficult to sing the Lord's song in the chapel when I recalled the USPG Chapel over the dungeon on the other side of the Atlantic. Like Jacob I wrestled with God that morning while the seminarians devotedly engaged in worship. I was astonished that the anguish feeling I experienced in the dungeon eighteen months ago had revisited me, but I was determined not to allow it to control me lest I too take up residence in the dungeon. Like the penitent psalmist who acknowledged his sin: "for I know my transgressions, and my sin is ever before me." (psalm 51: 3). I resolved to seek God's forgiveness for the cooperate sin of mankind. At the penitence the celebrant invited us to make our individual petitions. In the words of the hymn writer I silently prayed.

Dear lord and father of mankind, forgive our foolish ways!

Reclothe us in our rightful mind, in purer lives thy service find, in deeper reverence, praise.

The prayer was very comforting. Seeking forgiveness for the cooperate sin of the church and praying that we may be clothed in our rightful mind, for only then will we be able to offer true and laudable service to God. Then came the reassuring words of the absolution and the pronouncement of God's forgiveness.

Almighty God have mercy upon you forgive you all your sins

Through our lord Jesus Christ, strengthen you in all goodness,

And by the power of the Holy Spirit keep you in eternal life.

These words I have heard many times throughout my life. I myself as a priest have pronounced the absolution in God's name. But that morning as I knelt and heard that pronouncement it brought an entirely new dimension in my life. I went to the chapel that morning feeling somewhat troubled over the plight of our ancestors but I left strengthened to be an agent for change.

I shared my experience with the seminarians. I reminded them that while we cannot change the past it was incumbent on us to help change the narrative and God was calling them to prepare themselves for this formidable task.

The Anglican Church has had a long history of chaplaincy to the planters and at times became a part of the establishment. We should note that the Anglican Church in Barbados was disestablished from the state only in 1969. It is difficult to exercise our prophetic role when we are part of the establishment. Gratefully, in recent times the Anglican/ Episcopal Church has been addressing many of the social issues in our society.

The October 9, 2019 issue of the Christian Century published an article: "Episcopal seminary that benefited from slave labor creates reparations fund." The article stated that Virginia Theological Seminary (VTS) announced that it had set aside $1.7 million for a slave reparation fund. It is noteworthy that there are other institutions which benefited from slave labor, and have considered reparation, but have not yet implemented it. The article states VTS "was founded in 1823, and at least one of its buildings was built with slave labor. Black students were excluded from attending the seminary up until the 1950's." The article also acknowledged the Rt. Rev. Eugene Sutton, bishop of Maryland, who recently addressed congress on the subject of reparation. Before we begin to congratulate ourselves and become complacent, let us heed the reminder of Dr Kortright Davis in his book, "Emancipation still comin" Ironically, it was August 1st 2019, the anniversary of emancipation, that Dr. Clarke asked me to conduct the retreat.

Interestingly, Dr, Clarke stated that he too had visited Cape Coast Castle in Ghana and made the connection between the USPG Chapel over the dungeon in Ghana, and the Society Chapel for the slaves, that Christopher Codrington 111 had built not far away from the college.

Christopher Codrington was a man of great wealth and at his death in 1710 he bequeathed his two estates to the USPG. Provisions were made for the establishment of a college. The college provided a general education which included philosophy and divinity for the sons of the gentry. They would otherwise have gone to England for their education. The first graduate was ordained 1759. In 1830 the college began training candidates exclusively for ordination. Subsequently, in 1875 it became affiliated with the University of Durham in London and in 1965 the college became affiliated with the University of the West Indies. Sadly, Codrington did not visualize the end of slavery for he stated in his will that there should be at least three hundred slaves on the estate to provide the necessary labor. To his credit, however, we note that he insisted that the slaves should be educated, a rare thing in those days. His policy of amelioration of the poor whites and the slaves alienated him from the plantocracy and forced him to resign as governor of the Leeward Islands. Codrington made provision for a chapel to be built where the slaves could worship. Mention must also be made that the Codrington's family had also owned the island of

Barbuda. Incidentally, the capital of that island Codrington. The island was used chiefly for the propagation of slaves. Upon his death, Codrington bequeathed the land to the people of Barbuda. While they do not have a deed for the land, they enjoyed the freedom of occupying the land for several hundred years.

In conclusion, Christopher Codrington was a wealthy planter. He owned slaves but he left quite a legacy. There are many who believe that the education system in Barbados surpasses all the other Caribbean islands. This of course is primarily due to the foundation that Codrington had laid. Interestingly, two weeks after I returned from Barbados, one of the Sunday's lectionary reading was Paul's letter to Philemon. The recipient was a wealthy church leader and slave owner. In the letter the apostle persuasively encouraged Philemon to forgive and welcome back his runaway slave Onesimus. However, Philemon was asked to welcome the new convert as a brother in Christ. I wondered whether Christopher Codrington ever read Paul's letter to Philemon.

Our God did it again. Once more bringing some good out of evil. Yea! Even slavery. Christopher Codrington in his own way reached out and touched the slaves. Through his legacy he continues to touch the lives of others. Our God is like an artist who weaves the different the threads to make a beautiful tapestry. What an awesome God we serve! My pilgrimage to Africa would have been incomplete had I not gone to Barbados. Without the Barbados pilgrimage it would have been like an open-ended story. Like the Apostle Paul who insisted in going to Rome. I am happy that I had the privilege of reaching out to the seminarians. I hope that they would not get carried away with the perceived mystique associated with the priesthood but remain grounded to continue Christ's mission. I pray God will continue to touch them even through my feeble efforts. The seed has been sown. We wait for its germination and hope that they will bloom wherever God plants them.

Following our African pilgrimage, Enid and I traveled to Nevis. This was important. In a baseball game, a player must touch all the bases to score a run. Nevis is my home base. Having touched all the bases, including Ghana, I returned to home base.

One of the first things I did after returning home was to visit the graves of my grandfather, Joshua, and my parents. Standing at the feet of my father's grave, I remembered the day I left for seminary, some forty-seven years before. I remembered his long, strong, and powerful embrace. I remembered his unspoken words expressed in his embrace: "The hopes and aspirations of all the years are met in you, son, this day." I turned to my mother's grave and remembered her promise: "I will be praying for you."

It was important that I visit my parents' graves. Though long deceased, they have always played a special role in my ministry. In my first book, I wrote about an extraordinary experience I had on June 21, 1992, while presiding at the Eucharist for the first time in the new edifice. I was praying the Eucharistic Prayer:

"Sanctify them by your Holy Spirit to be for your people the Body and Blood of your Son, the holy food and drink of the new and unending life in him.… And at the last day bring us with all your saints into the joy of your eternal kingdom" (BCP, p. 363). Suddenly, I became aware that I was surrounded by the presence of my deceased parents I was in a state of awe. There was a brief pause. I regained my composure. Reflecting on that peak experience, borrowing Abraham Maslow's term, I concluded that my parents were proud of their son that morning. This gives credence to the Eucharistic words, "Therefore we praise you, joining our voices with angels and Archangels and with all the company of heaven, who forever sing this hymn to proclaim the glory of your name" (BCP, p. 362).

That indeed was a life-changing experience, and ever since then, whenever I preside at the Eucharist at St. David's and come to this part of the prayer, I immediately become aware of the mysterious presence of my parents. Sometimes, their presence is more noticeable than on other occasions.

In the weeks preceding my retirement as rector of St. David's, their presence was even more pronounced, especially when listening to the many tributes from parishioners. It was very difficult to maintain a dry eye.

As the days progressed toward my retirement service, I began to wonder how I was going to make it emotionally. On Sunday, March 24, 2019, Desna Dobson, Lynette Davson, and Sylvia Thomas gave tributes about my ministry. They touched the very core of my being. During the Eucharistic Prayer, I strongly felt the presence of my parents. I was completely choked up. Pauline Lovell, a Eucharistic minister, reached out to support me. I silently chided my parents, *Why are you doing this to me?*

Rose window

I regained my posture, and the service continued without any further incidents.

At the second service that day, all went well until the beginning of the recessional hymn. The choir, acolytes, and Eucharistic ministers assembled before the altar. Reverencing the altar in the usual priestly manner, I bowed and kissed the altar. Resuming my upright posture and facing the congregation, I glimpsed an unexplainable image in the left rose window, which immediately vanished. Raquiah Dixon, a Eucharistic minister, made eye contact with me, and suddenly, the floodgates were opened and the tears fell. I went straight to my office. I did not greet the parishioners at the receiving line at the end of that service. Strangely enough, that was the last time I felt the presence of my parents during worship at St. David's. What is even more remarkable, I had good control of my emotions for the remaining weeks of my tenure at St. David's.

Reflecting on this, I can truly testify that my parents accompanied me throughout my ministry. They supported me when I had the audacity to respond to God's calling to become a priest : a presumptuous hope. They accompanied me on that sacred journey in seminary. When I was thrown into the deep end of the pool, they were there and provided the buoyancy needed to help me tread water. They were there when I lived on the edge of parochial life's precipice. Their reassuring presence sustained me when I was tempted to quit and thus assisted me in becoming a part of the cutting edge.

What is amazing in this accompaniment, I was not always aware of their presence. I felt it strongly when I presided for the first time in the new building on June 21,1992. Now, if they were there for that celebration, it is reasonable to assume that they were there throughout the journey.

In the poem *Footprints in Sand*, the author writes about walking on the beach with our Lord. On reflection, she observed two tracks of footprints. Subsequently, they dwindled to one set, especially during the low periods of her life. She was told the tracks where she saw only one set of prints was where our Lord carried her.

Clarence and Alice, my parents, were like our Lord, walking on the beach with me; I was not aware of their accompaniment until they took their rightful place beside me at God's altar on June 21,1992. Thereafter, for almost twenty-seven years, they celebrated the Eucharist with us in the new building. And now, just before I officially ended my long tenure at St. David's, they exited the building. They assisted me to bloom where God planted me. In fact, they were co-creators with God, birthing me into this world. Then they became coworkers with God to ensure that I bloomed. We are reminded that God has no hands, no feet, but ours. Saint Augustine rightly said: "Without God, we cannot. Without us, God will not."

Before you dismiss this as mere superstition, remember that the Apostle Paul wrote about things seen and unseen. The things that are seen are temporal, he said, but the things that are not seen are eternal (2 Corinthians 4:18). The apostle added that we mortals are temporal, and at the resurrection, we will become eternal. This validates the unseen companionship of my deceased parents. They are like the wind. You cannot see them, but you can feel the effects of their presence. They are the wind beneath my wings, enabling me to bloom. They reached out and touched me in many ways.

After visiting my parents' grave, I then visited one of my surviving teachers. She was frail and in bed. She must have seen something in me and encouraged me to pursue my dream. I thanked her for her nurturing.

Because of her illness, she had not worshiped with her congregation for several weeks. After hearing that I was preaching the following Sunday, she made a giant effort to attend the service. She touched me in my formative years. Now I was touching her in her declining years.

At the Sunday's liturgy, I told the congregants of my recent pilgrimage to Ghana, where I visited the slave market and cemetery. On this sacred ground were two graves of former slaves who were exported to America and Jamaica. Their bodies were exhumed and brought back to their home country, where they were finally buried. On the same site were portraits of liberators of the African Diaspora, such as Dr. Martin Luther King Jr., Marcus Garvey, and W. E. B. Dubois. Also on the premises is a wall where visitors pay a fee to permanently inscribe their names. I told the congregation that while they may not be able to make that pilgrimage to Ghana, I inscribed my name symbolically on their behalf. I touched that wall on their behalf. Reaching out to the young people, I said, "I too journeyed where you are now traveling. I grew up and was nurtured in this church, in this community, and shared with them the words of an unknown author: 'It is not where you start; it is where you end up. You haven't failed until you stop trying.'"

I reminded them of our school's motto: *"Per Ardua Ad Astra"* (Through difficulties to the stars). Lastly, I visited Prospect Estate, where I once worked. It was the place where I made that radical decision, when I refused a government scholarship and answered God's call to the ordained ministry.

Returning to New York, Enid and I stopped in Antigua, where our ministry began. In our brief visit, we worshiped at St. George's Anglican Church, my first parish. This was the first time I sat in the building as a congregant. I had a feeling of nostalgia and reflected on my ten years of ministry in the parish: the many baptisms I administered, the numerous candidates I presented for confirmation, the many Eucharists I presided over, the numerous sermons I preached, the wedding ceremonies I officiated, and the funerals I conducted.

As I greeted the parishioners, I observed that some I once nurtured were now in leadership positions in the church and the community. This made me feel reassured that I had touched others in a positive way.

Over the past thirty-four years at St. David's, I had the privilege to administer the sacrament of baptism to 611 people; 191 people were presented for confirmation. I presided at thousands of Holy Eucharists. I preached thousands of sermons, officiated at 175 wedding ceremonies, and conducted 164 funerals. Hopefully, I did touch someone in these various ministries.

As Christ's liberators, we must constantly unwrap all the evils of religion and be clothed in the righteousness of God. Amos, the dresser of sycamore trees, was called to prophesy in Israel. He called for "justice to roll down like waters and righteousness like an ever-flowing stream." That call is still urgent today, for there are still many people living in the dungeons of our society: the homeless, the prisoners, the poor, the oppressed, the refugees, the marginalized, and the victims of racism, bigotry, and injustice.

The graves of two former slaves whose bodies were exhumed from Jamaica and the United States of America and were finally buried in the ancestral graveyard.

In my call from the grafting of fruit trees to the grafting of souls, I endeavored to preach many "how to" sermons of liberation. In so doing, I exhorted the listeners to remember Apostle Paul's words to the Galatians: "For freedom, Christ has set us free; stand fast therefore and do not return again to any yoke of slavery" (Galatians 5:1).

These sermons were not to suggest that God asked us to be successful. We are only called to be faithful. My long tenure in the ordained ministry had many glorious moments. It was also punctuated with hardships that often left me feeling as though I were in a dungeon. But as Apostle Paul said, "My grace is sufficient for you, for power is made perfect in weakness. So, I will boast all the more gladly of my weakness, so that the power of Christ may dwell in me" (2 Corinthians 12:9).

I have traveled the road, and I now prepare to finish the course. To paraphrase the words of the late Mahalia Jackson:

> I did try to help somebody, as I passed along.
> I did try to cheer somebody, with a word or song.
> I did try to show somebody that he's travelling wrong.
> Then, if I did, my living was not in vain.

What about you? Are you faithful to where God has planted you? Have you touched someone for the Lord? Are you living in such a way that your life will not be in vain?

APPENDIX

The Centurion as a Catalytic Converter
Mark 15:39

Mark 15:39 says, "So when the centurion, who stood opposite Him, saw that He cried out like this and breathed His last, he said, "Truly, this man was the Son of God!" So in line with our theme "Spiritual Tune-Up," I want to ask, "Are you a catalytic converter, like the centurion in Mark's Gospel?

What is a catalytic converter? If you are like me, you might have never heard of this instrument in your car. Back in 1975, the federal government mandated that all cars be fitted with these converters to transform harmful pollutants cars spit into the environment into less harmful emissions.

There are millions of cars on the road each day, spewing smog and pollutants. These are the main ingredients leading to acid rain, causing global warming, and even affecting our mucous membranes. The catalytic converter takes in these pollutants from the engine of the car and converts them into cleaner emissions. The catalytic converter, which is a simple, honeycombed surface instrument, pulls in the dirt, filters it, and then spits out cleaner air into the atmosphere.

How is the centurion in the reading like a catalytic converter?

First, let us look at who centurions were. A centurion was a trained soldier who had made his way up the ranks. He was known to be rough, course, cynical, and vulgar. He was trained to take orders and was cold, calculating, and cruel. At that time, the Romans stationed a legion of troops in Judea. These legions consisted of five thousand soldiers. For every hundred soldiers, there was a leader called the centurion. What did he do?

Described as the dirtiest job, the centurion was responsible for keeping the peace, preparing condemned criminals for execution, and carrying out the executions. In Jesus's case, this was execution by crucifixion, one of the most painful and cruel ways to die.

How did this centurion come in contact with Jesus? How did he become a catalytic converter? According to most biblical historians, chances are he already heard of Jesus prior to the crucifixion. In Matthew 8, we read the story of another centurion whose servant was gravely ill and paralyzed. When Jesus visited Capernaum, a centurion approached Jesus and asked for help. When Jesus asked him if he should go to his house and heal the servant, the Centurion said, "No Lord, just speak the word and my servant will be healed." He said, for I am a man of authority with soldiers under me. I tell one to go and he goes another to come and he comes; I say to my servant, "do this and he does it." He held much power and authority. However, because of his faith, his servant was healed!

Maybe this Centurion at the cross had heard of this miracle performed by Jesus, and so many more that Jesus had performed. He might also have been in Jerusalem, and witnessed, or heard about the crowds turning out to welcome Jesus, greeting him on as a king, throwing their garments on the ground and waving palm branches.

He might also have heard, or seen, the chief priests and teachers of the law angry with Jesus and asking Pilate to do something about it. Instead, Pilate turned Jesus back over to them. He might have been the one who gave the order to his soldiers to release Barabbas, instead of Jesus. Whatever the speculation, there he was standing, ensuring that the order to crucify Jesus was carried out! He saw how his own soldiers twisted a crown of thorns, placed it on Jesus's head, took his robes and wagered for it and finally mocked Him saying, "If you are the King of the Jews come down from the cross and we will believe you! You saved others, yourself you cannot save! Hail King of the Jews!" And finally, nailing Him to the cross, and piercing his sides to ensure that He was dead.

But it was there at the foot of the cross that the centurion witnessed and experienced something, a life-changing encounter, that led to his conversion from a callous centurion to a believer. He became a catalytic converter. All the dirt of ill-treatment of criminals, the politics of the time, the pollution of the hardness of his heart: everything was passed through that sift and purified. He recognized Jesus as the Son of Man.

What might have happened at the foot of the cross that made him declare Jesus to be the Son of Man? I believe it was what he saw and heard that changed his heart and led to his conversion.

That centurion stood at the foot of the cross and heard Jesus forgiving everyone, saying, "Father, forgive them, for they know not what they do." He told the thief, on his right side, "Today, you will be with me in paradise." These were life-changing words and experiences. But what that centurion saw after Jesus's death may have further impacted him, leading to his conversion. For the Bible tells us, "For from the sixth hour until the ninth darkness covered the face of the earth." Jesus cried out, "Father, into your hands I commend my spirit," and died. At that moment, the earth shook, rocks split, there was an earthquake, and everyone was terrified.

Maybe, in those moments, his life became dark and the world became unsteady under his feet. Matthew 27 speaks not only of the centurion but of the other soldiers who were there. All became terrified. The centurion, having witnessed this, declared, "Truly, this was the Son of Man!" That was the catalytic conversion.

Did others in the New Testament have similar conversions? Upon their encounter with Jesus Christ, all the dirt and baggage and toxins they were carrying around and spewing out were miraculously filtered and purified. Yes, we have many examples:

(1) When Saul was on his way to Damascus to kill the Christians, a voice asked him, "Saul, Saul, why are you persecuting me?" After that encounter, Saul was never the same again. He became Paul. one of the greatest converts for Christ.
(2) Jesus asked a woman of Samaria for a drink of water. He told her about her life: she had many husbands, and the man she was with now was not even her husband. She was shocked. But he offered her water, life-changing water, and she accepted it. She was converted and ran and told everyone about her encounter with Jesus.
(3) Do we realize that the thief on the cross on the right also experienced a catalytic conversion? Even at the point of death, his encounter with Jesus changed him instantly, and he was promised a place in paradise.

Let us look at ourselves now and ask, are we catalytic converters, like the centurion, or are we still emitting toxins into the air? Are we holding onto our toxins and not allowing the catalytic converter to do its job?

If we look at the story of the centurion at the cross, we realize that here was a nonbeliever, a Roman soldier, who was the first at the time of the crucifixion to acknowledge Jesus as the Son of God. Where were Jesus's followers? Where were his disciples, especially Peter, who claimed to love the Lord more than anyone else? Where was Judas, who betrayed him? Where was Thomas, who doubted him?

So it looks like from time to time, it takes an outsider to first acknowledge and recognize the Son of God. It's not usual for us, who sit in these pews every week, who come to church regularly to admit, with conviction, that this is the Son of God.

You see, we have been sitting here so long that we have forgotten what it means to have that new and sudden encounter with the Son of God. Have we become comfortable and complacent in our faith and lost the fire to emit clean energy into the world? Have our catalytic converters slowed down, or do we need new filters? Have we become complacent and failed to hold on to that encounter with Jesus that brought us here in the first place? In fact, have we become cold or lukewarm? In researching how a catalytic converter works, I learned that in order for it to be efficient, the car must be running for a while and the engine heated. That is why it is advisable to warm up your car's engine before you drive it. We are ineffective when we grow cold, just like the catalytic converter. We have to rediscover our fire for Christ and keep this encounter burning in our hearts. Where is our fire? What will it take to relight it? Has it gone completely out? How can we relight it? How then can we become converters if we are cold and our fire is out?

It is also important to be a catalytic converter by recognizing the wrongs in the world and speaking up or doing something about them. Our silence is deafening when we do nothing. Our silence around discrimination based on race, sexual preferences, prejudice, class, bullying, and male dominance, just to name a few. It is even worse when we are in positions to do something and choose not to get involved. We can correct so many wrongs in the world, starting right at our doorstep. We have been doing this by first, welcoming everyone who enters our doors at St. David's and making them feel as if they belong. Through our various ministries and outreach (e.g., HIV, health, music, and dance ministries, outreach to the sick and shut-ins). How do we comfort others during sad times? How do we share in each other's happiness? How kind and compassionate are we to each other?

Our priest, Father Nisbett, is challenging us to become change agents in the way we minister to those with mental health issues. There is a stigma and secrecy attached to those who are clinically depressed, for whatever reason; because of substance abuse, some people are now experiencing mental health issues. Others have Alzheimer's, dementia, bipolar, oppositional defiance, ADHD, and schizophrenia. Right here, right now, you or someone you know may be experiencing any of these. Can you be the catalytic converter to absorb the dirt and stigma attached to all these and filter them out through the right channels for help?

Finally, it is the encounter with Jesus at the foot of the cross that changes lives. It is there that the conversion occurs. Where were you when you encountered Jesus? Was it dramatic, like the centurion, or was it a slow realization over the years of who the Son of Man is? We must have that encounter, so as to bring our past and our baggage to him.

On the cross, Jesus took all that dirt and sin; he died for us so that we may experience life that is purer, happier, and anchored in him. Because of our encounter with Jesus, we have to bring the dirt, the pain, the hurts, and the disappointments to him at the foot of the cross and become the catalytic converter.

Historians say that after the centurion (and two of his comrades) encountered Jesus, he was baptized by the disciples and left the military. He left Judea and went to his native land, Cappadocia, to preach about Jesus Christ, the Son of God. He helped to spread Christianity and even saved the disciples from death, on one occasion. He was pursued by the Jewish elders, and under Pilate's order, he was finally beheaded. He is known as the Holy Martyr Longinus, the centurion who stood at the cross of the Lord.

Are you prepared to be a catalytic converter for Jesus Christ, like the centurion? Can you take the pollutants in your life, surrender them to Jesus, and leave here a better person, ready to serve, like the centurion? Only through a personal encounter with Jesus can this happen. When will you encounter Jesus?

Amen.

Lorna's meditation was one of seven given that day. By using the catalytic convertor as an example, the congregation was challenged mechanically. Concern for the environment was raised, but more importantly, our spiritual life was challenged. Four years later, she is still referred to as Ms. Catalytic Converter."

"You are a lucky young man. You were practically dead. The Lord must have saved you for a special purpose."

"I am offering you a government scholarship, which you have declined as you await something you are not sure about. Isn't that crazy?"

"The hope and aspirations of all the years are met in you, son, this day."

Are you asking me to be like Abraham? Is St. David's my Moriah? Is Jevon the Isaac whom you are asking me to sacrifice? Oh, God, please do not do that to us.

I wondered whether the bishop's prophetic words at the groundbreaking ceremony had come to pass. Anyone who thinks of building in New York City must be crazy.

How do you preserve the pregnancy and avoid a miscarriage? Above all, how do preserve your sanity?

God, are you still listening? Can you hear me? What are you up to now? Can I cooperate with you, or should I get out of the way?

I returned to the rectory just in time to stop another fire. In my rush to the job site, I forgot to turn off the burner on the stove. The kettle was almost destroyed, and the house was filled with smoke. Two fires in one day.

How can God plant me in such an oppressive church and expect me to bloom?

I could have easily said that Christianity is a white man's religion.

I was led to believe that all God had done in and through me was to empower me to help change the narrative.

ABOUT THE AUTHOR

The Very Rev. Joshua Mastine Nisbett, D. Min., was ordained to the priesthood in 1975. During his forty-four years of ordained ministry, he has served in only two parishes. His second pastorate lasted thirty-four years, despite tumultuous challenges at the outset.

His long tenure is largely due to his sense of vocational calling, his radical trust in God, his patience, his deep spiritual life, and his courage, like that of his namesake, Joshua. These virtues, along with his professional training, enhanced the growth and stability of his parish, St. David's. With much team effort, the congregation built and dedicated a new house of worship during the seventh year of his rectorship. With his leadership, the congregation adopted the principles of the Five-Star Church.

Nisbett also wrote *A Journey to the Promised Land*. Additionally, he has composed the lyrics to several hymns and wrote a Passion Play, *Who's on Trial?* in which he played the role of the main character, Jesus.

The author did much research work on the town of Cambria Heights and wrote about the early history of the town in his book. He has a doctorate in ministry from The University of the South, Sewanee, Tennessee. He earned a Master of Arts from Fordham University and Bachelor of Arts from the United Theological College of the West Indies.

CPSIA information can be obtained
at www.ICGtesting.com
Printed in the USA
FSHW011656041119